"*The Sacred Chase* unravels one of the most provocative stories found in the Bible. The man in Mark 5 named Legion overcame all odds and refused to use any earthly circumstance to get in the way of his deep longing to be free, whole, and auth̶̶̶ ̶ keen insights into the Bible, pov ̶iting style, Heath invites us to liv pro-vides practical, biblical way̶ lose to God as we want to be."

Mark Batterson, New ̶ ̶̶̶or of *The Circle Maker* and le̶ ̶̶̶ of National Community Church

"*The Sacred Chase*, encourages all believers to engage authentically with the unbridled pursuit of God's presence. God gives himself to us as an inheritance. Nothing is more astounding than that fact, and it demands a response on our part—pursue with passion. This pursuit is neither aimless nor vain. Jesus promised, 'I will be found by you.' Read this book and engage in the holy quest that reveals why we are alive."

Bill Johnson, Bethel Church, Redding, CA; author of *The Way of Life* and *Raising Giant-Killers*

"Heath Adamson is a prolific leader with a voice deserving to be heard. *The Sacred Chase* is a timely message for anyone who wants their life to count in a desperate world. Take the time to read this inspiring book and let it inspire you to greater things."

Hal Donaldson, president of Convoy of Hope

"Heath Adamson enters modern culture's chaotic arena with a clear call to let go of anything that may distract you from your God-given design to know and be known by your loving Father and to keep your eyes locked on the Author of your adventure on the earth. I highly recommend *The Sacred Chase* to anyone who is hungry to encounter the living God. You will not be disappointed!"

Kris Vallotton, leader of Bethel Church, Redding, CA, cofounder of Bethel School of Supernatural Ministry, and author of thirteen books

"Heath Adamson skillfully weaves compelling storytelling and impact-ful biblical truth to remind you there is limitless love available through Jesus Christ. *The Sacred Chase* invites you to authentically reflect on your pursuit of the God who calls you by name. Anyone interested in taking a step forward in their faith walk should read this book."

Rob Hoskins, president of OneHope

"Heath's latest book opens with Psalm 27:8: 'You have said, "seek my face." My heart says to you, "your face, Lord, do I seek."' What follows are inspiring reflections of contemporary and biblical stories that ignite our deepest longing to respond to the invitation to true intimacy with the One who created us—only to discover the God we seek has been in the chase all along."

Dr. Carol Taylor, president of Evangel University:

"Heath Adamson is a trusted gift. He has the voice of a Reformer. God is using his writings to free the church by reminding us of the things that matter most. Unquestionably there are many in the body of Christ who feel empty. The last two decades of passion and prosperity have not delivered. *The Sacred Chase* has come along at just the right moment to powerfully guide us back toward the pathways of righteousness."

Scott Hagan, president of North Central University,
Minneapolis, Minnesota

"Heath Adamson speaks with a voice of divine clarity, reminding us of what really lies at the end of the race of life—that the greatest pursuit of the human spirit is an encounter with the living Christ. Heath also reminds us that the chase is not ours alone. God began pursuing us long before we pursued him. In this book, Heath will engage you with the inspiration and spiritual authority of a man who has participated in and experienced the chase, and he will offer you insights through a lens of humility, grace, and transparency. I'm thankful for his friendship and that he continues to journal his journey with Christ on pages like these that are shared with the world."

Josh Skjoldal, lead pastor of Evangel

"Heath Adamson is such an incredible preacher and teacher of the Word. I am so thrilled that he's releasing this timely and relevant reminder that the demonic realm is real but Jesus is still our victory. Staying close to Jesus is essential, and in these pages Pastor Heath will help you in your walk with God. This book will bless you in a powerful way. Every believer needs to read *The Sacred Chase*."

David Hall, senior pastor and evangelist, Lifepoint Church,
Adelaide, South Australia

"In a world teeming with distractions, addictions, and obsessions that are all clamoring for our undivided attention, we need prophetic voices like Heath's to point us back to biblical truth. In *The Sacred Chase*, Heath challenges us to shake free from the temptations that threaten to pull us away from our calling in God and reminds us that the only person truly worth chasing in life is Jesus."

Rev. Samuel Rodriguez, lead pastor of New Season,
president of NHCLC, and author of *You Are Next!*

The Sacred Chase

MOVING FROM PROXIMITY TO INTIMACY WITH GOD

Heath Adamson

BakerBooks

a division of Baker Publishing Group

Grand Rapids, Michigan

Published by Baker Books
a division of Baker Publishing Group
PO Box 6287, Grand Rapids, MI 49516-6287
www.bakerbooks.com

Printed in the United States of America

Library of Congress Cataloging-in-Publication Data
Names: Adamson, Heath, 1977– author.
Title: The sacred chase : moving from proximity to intimacy with God / Heath Adamson.
Description: Grand Rapids, Michigan : Baker Books, a division of Baker Publishing Group, 2020. | Includes bibliographical references.
Identifiers: LCCN 2019046609 | ISBN 9780801093722 (paperback)
Subjects: LCSH: Spirituality—Christianity.
Classification: LCC BV4501.3 .A3335 2020 | DDC 248.4—dc23
LC record available at https://lccn.loc.gov/2019046609

Published in association with Creative Trust Literary Group, 210 Jamestown Park, Suite 200, Brentwood, TN 37027, www.creative trust.com.

20 21 22 23 24 25 26   7 6 5 4 3 2 1

To Ali.
I adore you and cherish our life together.
We are leaving a legacy for generations to come.

To Leighton and Dallon.
No eye has seen, no ear has heard, and no mind has
conceived what God has prepared for you.

To Bill, Beni, Kris, Kathy, Eric, and Candace.
From afar and up close, your pursuit of God's face has
compelled the Adamson family to hunger for more.
Your spiritual ceiling is becoming the floor for many.

To the team at Baker Books and also Creative Trust.
Thank you for the privilege of partnering with you.
I am grateful.

Most of all, to Jesus.
You capture our heart with a glance.

You have said, "Seek my face."
My heart says to you,
   "Your face, Lord, do I seek."

Psalm 27:8

Contents

Introduction

My childhood had its share of challenges. To balance them out, my time was filled with skateboarding, long bike rides, hours of basketball in the summer, sunburns, and playing video games with my friends. We didn't have earbuds, motorized scooters, or the internet. I grew up in a day when, if school might be canceled due to bad weather, there were no text messages or social media posts. We had to get up early, sit in front of the TV, and wait for the scrolling announcements at the bottom to see if our school was in session. There were no instantaneous directions because we didn't have maps on our cell phones. There were no cell phones. Parents drove down the highway without slowing down, with large paper maps in front of their faces to figure out where to go, while their young child held the steering wheel. Getting lost on trips was normal, just like riding up to the gas station to use the phone book was.

Every day we always found plenty to do to capture our imagination and expend our energy. But then the inevitable would occur. When young boys run out of sports to play, pizzas to eat, and dreams to chase, somehow and someway they find another adventure to go on. But there are some adventures that just aren't wise.

One day, as such a moment struck, I grabbed my fishing rod and headed to my friend's house. The fishing line needed to be strong as well as hard to see. For this reason, we rethreaded my rod with some line from his dad's tackle box. We happened to have a brand-new, crisp, fake twenty-dollar bill, and we used his mom's translucent tape to attach the currency to the end of the fishing line, tied a sinker a few feet away from the money, and walked down the alley to take the back roads to a small field filled with lush bushes and tall trees on one of the busiest streets in the neighborhood, next to the stoplight. The wind was nonexistent, which was perfect for our plan. We settled into the bushes and waited for about ten minutes to ensure no one had seen us walking down the street with the fishing rod.

We waited for the perfect moment, then I threw the fishing line out, and it landed exactly where we wanted it to. The fake twenty-dollar bill was lying right on top of the sidewalk, a few inches from the curb, and the fishing line was invisible. It looked like a twenty-dollar bill was lying on the sidewalk just begging for someone to pick it up. The bushes and trees were the perfect camouflage for us. We were able to observe everything that happened.

We watched, time after time, as people put their cars in park, turned on their hazard lights, got out, and walked over to the money. The unassuming victims of our boyhood menace knelt down, reached out—and we watched their faces as the fake money scooted away across the ground, thanks to our fishing contraption.

Then came one businessman in shiny shoes and dress slacks that he pulled up a bit as he knelt down, and that's when I slowly began to reel in the line. *The wind must have blown it*, I'm sure he thought. So he followed the money as it crept along the concrete. I started to reel the line faster as the man chased the money.

People were staring at him from their cars, and we laughed our heads off. Leaving an automobile with the engine still running at a stoplight is just foolish. Chasing fake money oddly crawling along the sidewalk is even more so. Our laughter quickly went beyond quiet snorts and chuckles, though we tried desperately to remain covert. It was just too funny!

What was equally as funny is that neither one of us stopped to realize that as I reeled in the line with the man chasing the money, I was also leading him right to us.

Before we knew it, we were face-to-face with a man whose forehead was covered with beads of sweat, whose dress shirt was soaked with perspiration, and whose face was twisted into a scowl.

As a young boy, I don't recall ever seeing an adult that angry before.

The man screamed at us and said words I'd had my mouth washed out with soap for—plus I learned a few new words that day. I grabbed my pole and my friend, and we ran away as hard and fast as we could through that field. The man never caught us and, once we arrived back at my friend's house safe and sound, we laughed that he'd never caught the twenty-dollar bill either.

The fake bill, that is.

That was the last time we played what we called "the money game." That was probably the last time that businessman dared to get out of his car to attempt to chase down a twenty in broad daylight too.

In Pursuit

We can laugh at this story, but the truth is we have all chased after something that had no real value at all, just like that fake twenty-dollar bill. We can be successful at what, in the end, doesn't even matter. We have also all pursued things that seemed good and valuable only to end up disappointed, rejected, or discouraged. Sometimes a college application is submitted but the resulting letter of denial disappoints us. We can apply for the job only to see it go to another candidate. A relationship we invested in can end not in greater connection but in heartbreak and betrayal. On the other hand, sometimes our pursuits in life do lead to accomplishing a few goals. Maybe our hard work pays off and we make some new friends, accumulate some achievements, or attain a promotion or two.

I am a firm believer in pursuing dreams and taking risks. There is certainly something special that takes place on the journey, whether the outcome is achieved or not. I am also a firm believer that there are no guarantees that every pursuit will end up the way we hope it will.

There is one pursuit we can go on, however, where our expectations and hopes are not only realized—they are exceeded. What pursuit is this? It is our pursuit of a deeper, sacred, more intimate connection with Jesus. This pursuit is not one of striving or begging; rather, it is one of inheriting and embracing. We chase the reality of God from a heart that is fully and finally at rest in Jesus. This deeper spiritual connection occurs by being authentic, intentional, and vulnerable with God.

There is a mind-blowing, never-ending connection with God available to everyone right now. I am not necessarily talking about meeting God so you can go to heaven after you die. That is of primary importance, don't get me wrong, for eternity is long, and your eternal salvation cost God all: his Son.

What I am referring to is the audacious pursuit of God and God's reckless love for you—what I call the sacred chase. Perhaps you can think of salvation in Christ like a door. Once you walk through that door, you will discover how unsearchable the love and promises of God are for you. For the difficulties ahead and for those moments of celebration, yes, but even more so for your every day. All of heaven desires to see your life soaked with the reality of God's presence. Pursuing this is worth all of your efforts. When deep connection and friendship with God is someone's desire, I have never seen that someone walk away disappointed.

Heaven Is Tangible Now

Although our lives should change when we meet Jesus, salvation is more than the transition from being a bad person to becoming a good person. When we receive the amazing gift of salvation, God performs the most remarkable miracle in our lives. Through salvation in Jesus, we literally go from being spiritually dead and eternally separated from God to being spiritually born into God's family.

Coming to faith in Christ, however, does not take away all of our problems. The baby's diaper still needs changing and children still get sick in the middle of the night. Water heaters still go out and an unexpected bill arrives in the mail—again. Flights may be delayed or canceled. Relationships don't always go as planned and, although the love of God is breathtaking, your mortgage company still requires you to pay on time.

When we are introduced to the goodness of God and all of his life-changing promises for us in Scripture, there can come a time when we see the object of our pursuit but it seems just beyond our grasp, just like that twenty-dollar bill. And in our striving and pursuing, we can become discouraged. We can even quit. We think holding in our hands the tangible expression of heaven on earth can happen for everyone—except us.

What we really need to take hold of is this: whenever we pursue a greater connection with God and endeavor to see the promises of Scripture become our very own, we always inherit the promise. How can I say that? That promise is not just an answered prayer or changed circumstance. Yes, God cares and is faithful. We should expect our prayers to be answered, and, if they are not, rather than excusing it away we press on and contend for the miracle. But the ultimate purpose of prayer is not just to get an answer.

The purpose of prayer and fulfillment of every promise, first and foremost, starts with God. God is our reward. God is at the beginning, the end, and the journey in between.

––––––––

Have you ever devoted your heart and soul to connect with God and felt like that connection was just out of reach? Or do you feel like God is hiding in the bushes as he dangles promises of hope, peace, a fresh start, strength for what lies ahead, healing in your relationships, miraculous divine turnarounds to situations, or direction for your future that he pulls further and further away from you?

Many if not all of us experience a tension between what we know to be true about God and our situation. This is not an excuse to become discouraged or to change our definition of God to fit our experience. This is a divine invitation.

Religious routine can easily replace the intimacy you used to have with God before life became busy and unpredictable. I can assure you the breakdown is not on God's end and the solution you need is within your reach. You can, and I believe you will, scoop up in your hand what your soul longs for.

Have you ever had a memory of something you did that made you feel ashamed and unworthy, or like God was mad at you? If so, you don't fully understand how God feels about you. Have you ever made commitments to read your Bible and pray, only to see your spiritual hunger fade? Yes, God is worth more of your heart, but rather than being disappointed with you, God is delighted in you for trying to connect with your Creator.

Do you want God to be more real in your life but are not quite sure where to begin or how to continue?

Does your past torment you? Does your future worry you? Is your present reality distracting you?

Has your lifestyle made it convenient to have a Christian-branded version of "you" but an empty, hollow soul?

Do you simply want to get closer to God? The reality of a spiritual life in full bloom, here and now, can begin. The choice is yours. God can't wait for you to start!

Now is the time, not to strive but to rest and to begin the most sacred of all pursuits and the most rewarding of all chases you can fathom.

There is so much more to your relationship with Jesus than you are experiencing.

God Chases Us First

You and I are as close to God as we want to be. We have all, like Moses, been invited to the top of the mountain to hear God's voice and walk down the jagged path of Horeb with tablets hand-inscribed by the very finger of God. Like Abraham, our days can be instantaneously interrupted by the One who invites us to journey into the unknown, looking for a city whose builder and maker is God, while remaining at peace, for what we do not see is much more real than anything we do see.

God beckons us all to step out on the water like Peter and watch heaven itself literally transform the physical world and make impossibilities like walking on water possible. When wisdom is needed for something we have never experienced, like Noah, God can provide the next steps for us to make informed decisions to bring our family through difficulty. When the shadow of the giant eclipses our face, and no one else around us knows how to break through that obstacle, like David, God knows where to find the smooth stones needed to take down our Goliath.

As a stay-at-home parent, you may feel insignificant and off of heaven's radar as you fold another load of laundry, clean up after another child, pay another bill, and talk to yourself since you're the only adult around. God is chasing you.

As a student, you may arrive home from school discouraged from the popularity game or hear the echo of the bully's words spoken about you. God spoke different words over you today you may be unaware of.

Perhaps as a single parent you struggle with the guilt of working multiple jobs to pay bills but not investing enough time with your children. God has a solution, and it is found in his presence.

Maybe you can no longer pretend, and your past is finally catching up to you. You may attend church regularly and feel like you're the only one struggling. You sit there, in quiet desperation, under the shadow of the steeple. God isn't angry with you. God loves you and invites you to the reality of heaven in your moment right now. Things can change.

You don't need to settle for anything less than what God promised.

Your finances may be tight, or you may have more than enough money to purchase a better brand of temporal, carnal misery. Your relationships may be shallow or nonexistent, or you may find yourself surrounded by healthy family and community.

Whether things are going great or you feel like you're stuck in a cycle of things constantly falling apart, *right now* is your moment to shout a resounding yes and begin the chase—the sacred chase—that always results in winning the prize. And what is that prize? The reality of Jesus in your life today.

This sacred chase is not about performing for God's approval; rather, it is about positioning your heart and responding to a divine glance. And one glance is all it takes.

CHAPTER ONE

Beyond Belief

Miraculously, not one person on her beach died that day. It was the day after Christmas, 2004. Around the world, families reminisced about their Christmas holiday in various ways. Parents recovered from the mental hangover of putting together the toys for their toddlers, which comprised thousands of tiny pieces and a small wrench spared by the manufacturer. (I am still convinced there is a conspiracy out there somewhere as drones hover outside of our windows and watch us struggle to put these toys together.) Ironically, by lunchtime the expensive toys requiring hours of assemblage are forgotten, and their cardboard boxes become the magical castle where the princesses dwell or the deep, dark, adventurous cavern where the superheroes spelunk.

Some spouses spent the holiday without the love of their life for the first time, because death comes to us all. Proud grandparents traveled back home after watching their grandchildren open presents and sitting around the table with their family. People all over the world ate fruitcake and wondered what in the world goes into it. Some students headed to the mall to return those denim jeans that were just a little too tight, probably a result of too many Christmas cookies. College students slept in. Some waitresses worked all day and would celebrate with their families later. Christmas music echoed in homes. For some, refrigerators were filled with leftovers from the holiday feast. Others couldn't afford the turkey or ham. New gloves adorned the cute little hands of the kids who were sledding, or new swimming trunks or swimming suits went on those who were surfing in the ocean.

Tilly's Beach

On that December 26, Tilly Smith and her family relaxed on the beach.[1] Their first family vacation had taken them to Thailand. Shortly after 8:30 a.m., ten-year-old Tilly, her parents, Colin and Penny, and her seven-year-old sister, Holly, went for a walk along Mai Khao beach, in front of their Phuket hotel. Disaster was the furthest thing from their minds. They enjoyed the warm breeze in their faces and felt the sand squish in between their toes. Fresh sea shells and creatures littered the beach.

A mere two weeks prior to their holiday, Tilly had learned about tsunamis in her geography class. As is the case with many ten-year-olds, Tilly did not find geography tantalizing, but the video her teacher showed had caught her attention. So, as Tilly and her family walked the beach, and she noticed the waves coming in but not going out, she dared to pay attention to something most people would have dismissed. Tilly had a different perspective that would soon change everything. The right information, applied at the right time, not only made a difference—it made *the* difference.

Tilly alerted her parents that they were surrounded by signs that something unusual, unexpected, and cataclysmic would occur. At first they were dismissive, but Tilly's passion and persistence paid off. She began shouting, "There is going to be a tsunami!" Now, what would you do if you were on vacation with your family and your ten-year-old daughter started screaming on the beach that a tsunami was about to strike? Imagine the embarrassment. Imagine what people thought. Breakfast on the beach interrupted by an irate ten-year-old is hardly vacation in my book. Tilly shouted louder and louder, and her panic frightened her younger sister, who began to sob hysterically.

Can you hear it? I imagine the volume increasing with her parents saying something like, "Tilly, are you all right? How can I help? Tilly, calm down! It will be okay. What's the matter with you? You're scaring your sister! Get yourself under control, now!" Tilly's dad took Holly back to the hotel to calm her down. Tilly and her mom walked on, but Tilly kept shouting. She looked around and saw the people in the ocean, on the sand, and just knew in her heart that everyone was in danger. Tilly then ran back to the hotel to find her dad conversing with a security guard.

"I know this sounds completely mad, but my daughter says there's going to be a tsunami," he said.

The security guard listened not to a PhD candidate, brain surgeon, or NASA scientist but to a passionate plea coming from a ten-year-old British schoolgirl. The guard listened to the most important voice—though it was disguised as a seemingly insignificant one—then shouted for people to get off the beach. Those in the pool began to run. Those in the ocean came to shore immediately and went to higher ground. People scattered all over the place as pandemonium set in.

It all happened so fast.

By this time, Tilly's mom was also running back to the hotel. She was one of the last people off of the beach. People screamed and children cried. Everyone was running. The hotel lobby, on a higher floor, became a gathering place. Then the reason for the pandemonium became evident. A tsunami, triggered by an earthquake at the floor of the Indian Ocean, struck.

This tsunami devastated nations. It killed an estimated 230,000 people.

Not one person from Tilly's beach died that we know of.

Tilly's dad, in shock after learning of the horrific devastation and suffering, said to Tilly, "What if we hadn't listened to you?"

What Tilly's father said is a logical thought, and one I would have as well. What if no one had listened to Tilly? I will take it a step further. What if Tilly hadn't listened to Tilly?

Believing Truth

When truth is no longer deafened by the voice of apathy, the results of our obedience, like Tilly's, are immeasurable.

What you believe and who you believe are crucial. In the end, this will determine the quality of your earthly life along with your eternal resting place (Hosea 4:6). There is a truth and, contrary to cultural opinion, truth is not relative. Truth is a Person whose name is Jesus. Whatever doesn't line up with the life and message of Jesus is inferior. Appearing to be authentic, it can simply be candy-coated poison. Just another fake twenty-dollar bill that takes our pursuit away from what is most valuable.

You can't always believe everything you think or feel. The heart is deceitful (Jer. 17:9). When you believe a lie, you empower it to produce results in your life. This is why Scripture says in Proverbs 23:7, "For as he thinks within himself, so is he" (TPT). The Hebrew word translated "think" means to "calculate, estimate, put a valuation on." It is safe to say that what we calculate to the thousandth decimal in our thinking, which takes place often subconsciously, literally shapes how we perceive the world. There are more electrical impulses traveling from your brain to your eyes than vice versa. This means your brain tells your eyes what to see.

When you believe the truth, it opens a door for freedom to reign (John 8:32). Believing the truth, however, is not enough to experience the freedom God created you to experience. James 2:19 says, "You believe that God is one; you do well. Even the demons believe—and shudder!" The Passion Translation puts James 2:19–20 this way:

> You can believe all you want that there is one true God, that's wonderful! But even the demons know this and tremble with fear before him, yet they're unchanged—they remain demons. O feeble sons of Adam, do you need further evidence that faith divorced from good works is phony?

What is the big idea? Tilly took what she believed and did something with it. It took courage for her to live out what she knew to be true, though she might be misunderstood or criticized, as everyone else around her did not see what she saw. She was vulnerable, allowing her beliefs to move her outside of her comfort zone to a place of decisive action regardless of how inconvenient it was. She stood alone.

When Believing the Truth Isn't Enough

Believing in the truth isn't enough. Had Tilly believed a tsunami was about to strike and remained silent, the miracle of Mai Khao beach would instead have been a tragedy. Although what you believe is of life-or-death importance, what you do with that belief is equally if not even more significant. If we say we believe but it does not transform our motives, deeds, and priorities, we are simply chasing a twenty-dollar bill that we will never be able to spend down the sidewalk.

People often ask, "Do you believe in God?" It is an important question and one that can unlock our purpose. The intent of this book is not to convince you to believe in God; instead, I want to convince you that *God believes in you* and *there is a relationship with God that is beyond belief.* If you dare to believe God's invitation to "have life and have it abundantly" (John 10:10) and allow that belief to move you to a place apart from all excuses, all mistakes, all areas of shame, and all of the reasons you think you have to justify why your audacious pursuit of God's goodness in your life won't work, you will never regret it.

Never.

In John 10:10, the Greek word translated "life" can mean "the state of one who is possessed of vitality."[2] Can you imagine your life literally being possessed by vitality? In the same verse, "abundantly" means "continuous and excessive."[3] The word picture of this sort of life would be a cup so full that it is overflowing and, though it drips all over the counter and onto the floor, the source just keeps pouring and pouring and pouring. You may think it is waste; God says it's life.

If I told you I was giving you twenty-five million dollars, after your bewilderment went away and you realized it was actually true, immediately your dreams of how to spend the money would begin. Houses, cars, vacations, shopping, charities, school bills, and the like would be glad recipients of your new-found wealth. You may not receive twenty-five million dollars, at least not from me, but you have an inheritance worth much more than this. It is found in a relationship with the God who knows it all, sees it all, and still absolutely loves you. Your soul will thank you one day if you go looking for your inheritance in Christ. It isn't far away, nor is it buried deep beneath the ocean's surface. Your spiritual inheritance is found by gazing into the eyes of God, knowing true love, and embracing the authenticity found only in that space. God is your inheritance, and the abundant life with him should never stop flowing. Sometimes, unfortunately, it does, when our perception overshadows how good God really is. What we perceive can be self-fulfilling, and it isn't God's fault. Without a true glimpse of Jesus, we can tolerate the inferior and counterfeit in our lives.

The Power of Hope

In the 1950s, a professor at Johns Hopkins named Curt Richter conducted an experiment with rats (both domesticated and wild) that were placed in jars filled halfway with water. The domesticated rats were placed inside one by one, and the amount of time they swam around was measured. The first rat swam incessantly and then dove to the bottom of the jar, where it placed its nose up against the glass and continued swimming. After about two minutes, that rat died. Nine other domesticated rats did something quite different: they swam for days before giving up.

The wild rats, recently trapped, aggressive, and known to be good swimmers, surprised Dr. Richter. All thirty-four of them quit within a few minutes of being placed in the jars. He then tweaked the experiment. In the first experiment, the rats did not experience fight or flight; rather, he said, they experienced hopelessness. In the second experiment he sought to create a scenario that wasn't hopeless. Watching closely, he picked up the rats just before they stopped swimming, held them briefly, and then placed them back in the jar. And that brief moment of time the rats were removed from their striving in the water made a difference.

The rats that experienced a break from their struggle swam longer and lasted longer than those that were never held. Dr. Richter believed the rats kept swimming when they had a reason to. A *Psychology Today* blog post puts it this way: "There are obviously many differences between humans and rats. But one similarity stands out: We all need a reason to keep swimming."[4]

When we go on the journey with God and live our life with Jesus, life can feel like a struggle at times. We may not even feel like we are making much progress in our God-connection. The abundant life God promised seems too good to be true—at least for us. But what I am learning is that we don't have to wait for God to reach down and give us a reprieve from our swim. The rest we need is within us, for that is where our great God lives. But for many of us it just doesn't feel that way all the time, does it? Is there anything God can do about the gap you experience between the divine promise and your current reality? You may think, *I sure hope so*. But remember, God already took the necessary steps for you to inherit every promise provided to you and all generations to come. The next step, which is possible and doable, is up to you.

Like Tilly's, your situation is perfectly designed for truth and belief to meet wholehearted devotion.

The Bible is full of examples where individuals, refusing to be distracted from their purpose in knowing God in a deeper way, laid aside baggage from their past, excuses from their present, the illusion of success, and anxieties about their future to go on the sacred chase. In Matthew 20, the blind beggars cried out desperately to Jesus of Nazareth, who was walking by on the Jericho road. They were told to calm down and be quiet, yet they shouted even louder. Jesus stopped and looked at the blind men, not the first time they cried out but the second time. This tells me that sometimes our condition will capture the heart of God while at other times our spiritual passion will. I wonder what would have happened if they'd stopped crying out when the crowd told them to be quiet? Have you ever cried out to God before and decided not to cry out a second time?

Job, a righteous man whose family and wealth were tragically taken from him, had every reason to be cynical toward God. Job chose to walk humbly and remain devoted to God. Rather than accusing God, Job was led by his pursuit to say, "Though he slay me, I will hope in him" (Job 13:15). What is Job communicating? We can infer he meant his passion for God would never be subject to his earthly circumstances.

Queen Esther devoted herself for months, in preparation, to stand before her earthly king and defend the marginalized. Elijah outran chariots. Paul endured prison. David stood firm in the face of intimidation. The man they called Legion, whom we will learn later had a multitude of excuses, chose to let his love for God slay every one of them. Abraham, "in hope . . . believed against hope" (Rom. 4:18). Hope is a powerful force, and when we allow ourselves to hope for the reality of heaven to emerge in our lives on the earth here and now, we will never be disappointed (Isa. 49:23).

In our age, style is often exalted over substance. Spiritual apathy can easily take on the appearance of what we call "balance." What we see, and the way things appear, can lure us into an illusion. God is not impressed with performance. God looks at the heart (1 Sam. 16:7) and searches far and wide for someone who will wholeheartedly commit themselves to the sacred chase (2 Chron. 16:9). This reaches further than coming to God with our problems in prayer. If the problems in our life went away, would we still have a prayer life?

Seeking God with our whole heart is revealed when we want divine connection more than anything else. Can we come to God in prayer and trust our good Father cares, answers, and meets our needs? Of course. Philippians 4:19 reveals that God supplies our needs. It is possible, however, to get so caught up with a lot of other things that we miss the most important thing. Matthew 6:33 says, "But seek first the kingdom of God and his righteousness, and all these things will be added to you." You can seek things and forfeit the kingdom. When you seek the kingdom, everything else comes with it. I pray my, and your, dominant fixation in life is simply to catch a fresh glimpse of who God is again. Day after day.

Our examples of Job, Esther, David, and the rest reveal a common thread: they all bent their hearts in God's direction. They chose inheritance over convenience. What do I mean? One of the most remarkable promises God makes to us is found in Ephesians 3:20: "[God] is able to do far more abundantly than all that we ask or think, according to the power at work within us." In this verse we see that not only is God able, God is willing. This reveals a significant truth for you and me: all of this mind-blowing, dream-shattering goodness of God displayed in our lives is somehow, some way, related to the condition of our souls.

The word "power" in Ephesians 3:20 can be literally translated "dynamite."[5] The phrase translated "according to" is the Greek word *energeó*, meaning "to work or accomplish."[6] This is where our word *energy* comes from, which can literally mean "an electrical current energizing a wire." It's almost as if all of God's goodness and your spiritual inheritance are packaged in a stick of dynamite, and you have the ability to light the fuse. This affects your marriage, children, friendships, family lineage, finances, emotional and physical health, destiny, purpose, and entire life. With no spark, the dormant power is useless. The words "according to" reveal that much of the quality of our spiritual lives is not up to God; it's up to us.

One Door Takes Us There

A detailed study of the New Testament reveals dozens of reasons why God sent his Son to earth. I am thankful for one of the most well-known, widely recognized reasons: salvation. When God became tangibly real to me at seventeen, and I discovered how deep and rich the grace of God is, it seemed far too good to be true. I was and am eternally grateful for salvation. The lifestyle I was rescued from is proof that God restores. Jesus is more real now than ever. Although my salvation through Jesus Christ still takes my breath away, it wasn't until I had walked through that door that I began to realize how wide and deep and high God's love is. I then began to notice the other reasons Jesus came. One of them is to consistently grow us in our understanding of God's love.

The apostle Paul expressed it this way in Ephesians 3:17–19: "That you, being rooted and grounded in love, may have strength to comprehend with all the saints what is the breadth and length and height and depth, and to know the love of Christ that surpasses knowledge, that you may be filled with all the fullness of God." Love is a Person (1 John 4:8). Without Christ, we cannot know God.

Through Christ and our salvation in him, the most unbelievable privilege and reality in the universe become ours. We can know God intimately and personally. I am thankful for eternal life (John 3:16), but I am equally thankful for the ability to know God in this life too. Paul invites the Ephesians, and through these Scriptures the Holy Spirit invites us too, to "know the love of Christ which surpasses knowledge" (Eph. 3:19). How can you know something that surpasses being known?

You have just officially learned about the sacred chase.

In this verse, we have a divine invitation to let loose our deep, pent-up hunger for God and point every area of our lives in God's direction. God put eternity in our hearts (Eccles. 3:11) and also invites us to search for the unsearchable (Prov. 25:2). We have a deep longing to see the Unseen One, though we may not always feel that way. It is almost as if God says, *Hey, there is no way you will ever know, understand, or even begin to figure out how crazy I am about you. But go ahead and try! I will enjoy every second of it. I have been waiting for this moment since long before you were born.*

Yet somewhere along the line, thousands of voices begin talking us out of our divine design to start and finish our sacred chase. We can fill our lives with pleasure, accolades, and getting "more," only to realize in the end we confused our goals with God's purpose.

Our busy lives keep us going, just enough, to avoid the necessary stillness needed to hear the divine whisper. Are we afraid of what God may show us in the silence? Henri Nouwen thought so when he said, "There was a time when silence was normal and a lot of racket disturbed us. But today, noise is the normal fare, and silence has become the real disturbance."[7]

We compromise and call it tolerance. We slowly let the very things that used to destroy us creep back in and call it authenticity. We don't want to be "religious and legalistic" and can therefore justify the dimly burning spiritual flame in our heart. We can neglect ancient, timeworn spiritual disciplines that are sure to bring spiritual health because we become addicted to the next new thing. We can ignore reading and studying Scripture because we listen to a sermon every now and then. We tolerate the very things that destroy lives and call it entertainment.

Now, there is nothing wrong with having goals, purchasing a house, going back to school, or watching a movie. I am not talking about selling it all, moving to a monastery, living off of rainwater and berries, or saying adios to technology. It is God who gives us the knowledge, wisdom, and understanding to create the computer chip, build the skyscraper, or pilot a plane to take families to their favorite vacation destination. And that's exactly my point. It is God.

We can become like the older brother in the parable of the prodigal son in Luke 15 and take advantage of God's goodness by becoming content with the father's blessings without desiring to spend time with the father in his house. In this way, unfortunately, we treat God like a mere prostitute, where intimacy is exchanged for mere want. The younger brother was seduced by opportunities that ended up becoming distractions from what eternally mattered. Only after the younger brother became impoverished did he realize true, unending wealth was found in simply being present with the father.

The only rational commitment you and I can make to Jesus, given he laid down his life for us, is complete and total surrender to live a life of love and devotion to God (Luke 9:23).

One Step

Do you need to grow in your connection with God? If you say yes, then this book can help you immensely on that journey. You can fuel your passion for God and know unknowable love. If you respond, "No thanks, I am just fine where I am," then I pray you continue reading, for maybe there is much more available and accessible to you as a follower of Christ than you first believed or were taught. Regardless, the difference between "God is nowhere" and "God is now here" is something small, insignificant, and achievable by everyone. The difference is one simple step.

Once you begin the sacred chase, your challenges in life become smaller as your perspective of God's love and goodness become clearer. The sacred chase for the heart of God will help you become the spouse and parent you were created to be. It will bring freedom from your past to your mind once and for all. It will grant you the wisdom to know which decision is best. It will equip you to distinguish between confrontation and conflict and learn how to establish boundaries in relationships when necessary. It will benefit your business and bless your life. None of these things are the ultimate prize, however; God is. If knowing God was the only reward for a life of commitment to Jesus, then that reward is worth it.

In the midst of opportunities that seduce us, excuses that paralyze us, and experiences that often confuse us, we have a longing deep within our soul for more of God. There is a primal hunger for God that this world can never fully and finally satisfy, yet our faulty understanding of God and the distractions of this life often sabotage us from starting.

Two verses in Hebrews 12 seem to capture it all:

> Therefore, since we are surrounded by so great a cloud of witnesses, let us also lay aside every weight, and sin which clings so closely, and let us run with endurance the race that is set before us, looking to Jesus, the founder and perfecter of our faith, who for the joy that was set before him endured the cross, despising the shame, and is seated at the right hand of the throne of God. (vv. 1–2)

Hebrews 11 is full of the stories of ordinary people like us whose sacred chase often included unusual circumstances and unlikely destinations. Through challenges like the inability to conceive children, dysfunctional families, insurmountable trials, physical pain, and spiritual ups and downs, they continued to run their race to win their prize.

After being inspired and encouraged when we read Hebrews 11, we find chapter 12 drives a stake in the ground. The writer provides an illustration we can all relate to, if not personally then certainly through what we have watched on TV. The word translated "race" in Hebrews 12 is also used in ancient Greek literature to describe athletic games, even the original Olympus games from which the modern Olympics are patterned. That word is *agon*, from which we also derive our word *agony*, and it refers to the strenuous training and competition the athletes endured in the games. It is also used in ancient literature to describe a struggle in the human soul.[8]

Scripture is painting this picture of you and me in a large arena, surrounded by some who want us to win and others who want us to lose. It is up to us to compete to win. To do so, we must make sure we aren't weighed down with anything, and we put away or literally "renounce" all types of sin. The word translated here as "sin" can mean "a brand of sin that is self-originated."[9] The struggle in our soul can be won when we let go and throw away anything that distracts us from our prize. We are then instructed to let our gaze fall on Jesus who is our author (literally "pioneer") and finisher.

You can run your spiritual race with all of your heart, but if you are running in the wrong direction, you still won't finish.

————

By now, you may be thinking that the sacred chase refers to doing more Christian things like reading your Bible, praying, going to church or life group, or giving financially. These can be healthy things, but as we will see, they are symptoms of a race well run, not necessarily proof of it. Judas Iscariot, the one who betrayed Jesus, basically did all of these things. He was not a hypocrite. Judas was an unbeliever. Judas didn't lose his relationship with God at the end of his life. It appears from the Gospels he never had one. In Greek literature, when the writer describes an event and a list of names appears, the order of those names is significant. Typically, the first name is considered the most prominent or relevant to the reader. Judas's name appears about twenty times, and usually it's in a narrative where other disciples are also mentioned. He is always mentioned last. It is almost as if one of the most well-known of all Jesus's followers is unfortunately, due to the condition of his heart, a dark horse.

To run well and finish strong, you must first take an honest assessment of where you are in your connection to God and how you got there, and make a commitment that you are going to accept once and for all that God is worthy of your pursuit.

We can spend a lifetime finding blame for the reasons we live beneath God's best, or we can look to Jesus and let God show us where to really begin. John 3:34 tells us God "gives the Spirit without measure." Who sets the limits? The devil doesn't. Our culture doesn't. Our past doesn't. Our race, gender, or social status doesn't have to.

The limits are up to you and me, within the condition of our soul, for there is a spiritual inheritance in Jesus that can be claimed only one person at a time. This is the moment for each of us to take what we believe, like Tilly did, and apply it to our situation. If what we believe is correct but is overshadowed by apathy, our spiritual adversary doesn't need to speak to us or tempt us anymore. But if we take what we know to be true about God's goodness and allow our spiritual passion to overtake our other priorities, the words of Job will become ours: "I had heard of you by the hearing of the ear, but now my eye sees you" (Job 42:5).

CHAPTER TWO

Stained Glass and Starry Nights

There is one enemy of our sacred chase that often remains undetected. It causes us to become impressed with ourselves and, though we're slowly decaying, provides an appearance of life. Spiritual apathy wears it like a costume. We will call it *proximity*. It appears real but is inauthentic. It does not require intentionality for it is based merely on convenience. It detests vulnerability for this is how its lie is exposed. Proximity, also called *nearness*, *religious performance*, or *lack of vulnerability*, is a shrewd enemy of our spiritual inheritance. It is cloaked with the trappings of the Pharisee, the selfish churchgoer, the unbelieving saint. Eugene Peterson captures the essence of this in his book *The Jesus Way*, where he says:

> Religion is one of the best covers for sin of almost all kinds. Pride, anger, lust, and greed are vermin that flourish under the floorboards of religion. Those of us who are identified with

institutions or vocations in religion can't be too vigilant. The devil does some of his best work behind stained glass.[1]

I discovered how easy it is to confuse proximity and intimacy with God in a cold, dark place underneath the cobblestone streets of Jerusalem. This is where I began to understand how, in the midst of even the most holy of places and among the most religious of people, we can think we are close to God only to be, in reality, deceived.

It was my first time in Jerusalem. I was there for some work-related meetings. We had a few hours to spare, so a coworker arranged for a resident of the city who was a history scholar to take us around. We stood on the Mount of Olives and walked through Gethsemane. It was important to me that, during our brief time together, we didn't go to the traditional sites. I wanted to see historical sites. In ancient times, when a city was conquered, the invading army razed the city and built on top of it. To walk the streets Jesus of Nazareth would have walked, one must often look below the ground.

Underneath the streets, we walked among ruins of a residence from first-century Jerusalem that was being excavated by archaeologists. It would have belonged to a religious official. I remember seeing some of the mural work on the floors and a ritual cleansing area. I was surprised at how large it was. For some reason I assumed everyone who served in a religious position was poor during that era. I was sadly mistaken.

The powerful and affluent lifestyle of the religious leaders was laden with greed, was corrupt, and often served to make the rich richer and the poor poorer. God's story was told in the synagogues, the temple, and often over meals by some of these leaders, but God was nowhere to be found in their stories.

Our historian friend helped us understand that a sect within Judaism at the time of Christ, known as the Sadducees, was the priestly caste and created an economic enterprise with the help of the Romans and Herodians (a family dynasty of Herod the Great charged by the Romans to keep the peace in Palestine). The caste centered around a sacred place, known as Herod's Temple, and a small, silver coin known as the Tyre coin. The temple tax, something all devout Jewish believers paid, had to be paid with the Tyre coin. And the priests controlled the price of the tax. Corrupted by power and greed, the religious system that initially represented purity, humility, forgiveness, and the worship of God became an economic engine used for corrupt gain by a select few. We were told that many people could not afford to give sacrifices any longer as the taxes were raised by the caste. People felt rejected by God because they couldn't meet the expectations of the religious system. They felt guilty and ashamed because they just couldn't "do enough."

I was shocked to hear our guide say that some of the priests who were not part of the corrupt elite even starved to death because the religious leaders wouldn't share revenues. Just imagine hearing the story of God come from someone who lived in a mansion while other priests starved. I can assure you God is nowhere to be found in religious pretension like this.

How could they forget the Person the story was all about? How could they sit by, as expert storytellers, and fail to whole-heartedly insert themselves into the story? I have a feeling nothing makes God angrier than telling the wrong story about him.

I thought of Luke 2, when twelve-year-old Jesus went to the temple with his parents, and Mary and Joseph lost him. Who loses the Son of God? Ironically, Jesus was lost not in the prison where "bad people go" or the part of town where "sinners hang out," but in the temple, where God's presence supposedly resided. I wonder, do we ever lose God in the places he should be found, like our marriage, thought life, dating life, decisions, finances, or goals?

One reason Jesus came was to change our minds about who God had become to the soul of humanity. Jesus took the greatest commandment from the Old Testament, which was to "love the LORD your God with all your heart and with all your soul and with all your might" (Deut. 6:5) and added a word. Mark 12:30 says, "You shall love the Lord your God with all your heart and with all your soul and with all your mind and with all your strength." The word *mind* was added. Why?

What we think and how we think about God changes everything. As we pursue a deeper connection with Jesus, who we understand him to be determines our response to him. The word *repent* can literally mean "to change the way you think."[2] He came to invite us so close that, as we gaze into his face by prayer, Scripture reading, fasting, worship, surrender, humility, conversation, and a multitude of other practices, made possible by grace alone, we see a true reflection of who we really are in his eyes.

Jesus looked at a large crowd of people who were familiar with God through religion and declared his "burden" to them all. What did Jesus say to those who had a cloak of religion? "The time is fulfilled, and the kingdom of God is at hand; repent and believe in the gospel" (Mark 1:15). Jesus invited them to exchange all they devoted themselves to with something much more superior: intimacy with God. For example, lepers in the first century were quarantined and isolated from society, and it was against Jewish law to come in contact with them. How did Jesus heal the leper? Jesus touched him. In Mark 5, we see another invitation from Jesus to the religious who lacked true intimacy with God. A woman had been bleeding for twelve years. I once had a medical doctor describe to me what her physical appearance could have looked like, and he believed she could have weighed approximately eighty-five pounds.

She'd lost all she had, according to Mark, and certainly lived with the stigma of poverty and isolation. It was against Jewish law to come in contact with a woman in this condition. In front of the large crowd full of religious leaders, Jesus not only healed her but called her "daughter." Those whom religion avoided Jesus loved.

Now we know why Jesus was full of emotion when he introduced his ministry to the residents of first-century Jerusalem with a whip and by flipping tables. This isn't exactly what you would expect from meek and mild, loving and compassionate Jesus.

Tables and Coins

Matthew 21:12–13, Mark 11:15–19, and Luke 19:45–47 record Jesus driving money changers out of the temple toward the end of his brief public life. However, the Gospel of John (2:12–22) records Jesus doing something similar at the beginning of his public ministry, but John clearly describes a different account than the other three Gospels. On two separate occasions, Jesus went into the temple area and caused quite the scene. Jesus began and finished his public life with similar displays of intolerance toward the abuse of power and misrepresentation of God only religion can afford. Knowing what we now know about this small group of corrupt leaders, whose hunger for wealth at any cost polarized true spiritual believers and starved

41

priests who had pure motives, we understand why Jesus said what he said.

Jesus used a whip of ropes, shouted at religion, caused the animals to be loosed and run wild, and flipped coins to the ground that were used to misrepresent the heart of God. He would have broken money boxes and exposed the corrupt leaders for who they truly were. Jesus thundered, "Take these things away; do not make my Father's house a house of trade" (John 2:16). Those around would have recognized this as a reference to Psalm 69:9: "Zeal for your house has consumed me, and the reproaches of those who reproach you have fallen on me." Later on, Jesus would speak again of the hearts of the corrupt leaders by saying, "This people honors me with their lips, but their heart is far from me; in vain do they worship me" (Matt. 15:8–9).

I learned something else that day underneath the ground in Jerusalem. Not only was the religious system corrupted by a few powerful leaders and the heart of God misrepresented in a religious system, but the location of the tables Jesus flipped over is crucial to understand. The temple mount, approximately thirty-five acres in size, served as the foundation for the temple. Only priests could enter the temple, which, compared to the three courts surrounding it, was rather small in size. Israelite men could enter the court closest to the temple, while both the men and women of Israel could enter the middle court. Only Jews could pass through certain courts to go and fulfill the necessary requirements for their sin to be atoned for. A non-Jew, or gentile, was only allowed to enter the Courtyard of the Gentiles, which was farthest from the temple. A sign was posted warning gentiles that, if they passed through a certain entrance, their crime against the religious system was punishable by death.

The tables where animals were purchased for sacrifice were set up in this Courtyard of the Gentiles. Selling animals for sacrifice was not the sin (see Lev. 5:7). Jesus did not just react; he proactively responded to the misrepresentation of the story of God in front of both Jews and gentiles. The corrupt religious system, set up by a handful of leaders who were greedy and loved money, inhibited God's house from being a place of prayer, or simple conversation with and relationship to God.

Proximity and Intimacy

Many of us confuse proximity to Jesus with intimacy with Jesus. God did not send his Son into the world so we could have something else to do on Sundays. Jesus came because apart from him all of life's experiences, successes, failures, and memories are merely temporal, insignificant in light of eternity, and therefore illusory and figments of our imagination. Religion can create some of the most hollow souls, where we learn to speak about God as if he is not even in the room any longer. As in Revelation 3:20, Jesus can stand at the door of his own house and knock, while we can sit at his table, feast on his blessings, and not even notice he is no longer found in our religious routines. If we heard Jesus knock and opened the door, I wonder how many of us would be surprised to see him and say something like, "Jesus, I am sorry you had to knock! I guess I never noticed you weren't in your house, at your table, with us."

In our culture, *religion* is a word often used to describe the object of our cynicism or our disdain for hypocrisy. More people are less committed to the religion they inherited or were taught than their parents were. People say things like, "I like

Jesus but I just don't like religion," or they confuse devoting their life to standards of truth with something negative like "being religious." Being conservative is not the same as being holy and pure of heart. Some of the most conservative followers of religion falsely accused Jesus of Nazareth of moral compromise when he demonstrated unconditional love. Religion is often blamed for extremism and the dark moments in our history like the Crusades, genocide, or colonialism. I completely understand where some people, turned away by religion's hypocrisy, are coming from. Some of these perspectives about religion are unfortunately true.

In our hypersarcastic and cynical world, religion does not have to be negative. When the heart's motivation is to love God and love others according to the greatest commandment, humanity partners with the divine to pull heaven to earth. By definition, religion is an attempt to organize beliefs, traditions, symbols, and practices so we can share them with others in our family and community.

Christianity emerged as a community of people who loved Jesus. When an epidemic plague beginning in AD 165 claimed the lives of up to a third of the Roman Empire's population, early Christians cared for those abandoned to die. It is because of this love and compassion that many believe the Christian church stood out as a representative of the authentic, true God.[3] Eventually, there was need to organize beliefs to preserve the essence of Jesus's teachings and actions. I am grateful we have these preserved today. We can thank the "concept" of religion, or the organization of beliefs and traditions, for this.

During the Middle Ages the religion of Christianity brought hundreds of churches to Europe that welcomed the sick, dying, castaways, outcasts, and marginalized. Religious people are more likely to give money and volunteer. It is because of religion that something special is in the air in December when, regardless of one's beliefs or faith orientation, the importance of generosity and giving is more noticeable. Religion provided the first hospitals on earth, many organizations that partner with others to end physical and spiritual poverty, and language and experience to pass on deep beliefs to our children's children.

I often hear people, as I speak and travel, talk of their search for authentic spirituality and religion. They want to walk with God because, in their hustle and bustle of life, nothing else seems to be capable of awakening and satisfying their soul.

Do you think there must be something wrong with you or, perhaps, that God is not interested in you? Maybe you look at your efforts to know God, live a good life, and do the right thing and still feel as if you come up short. Richard Rohr puts it this way: "Religion is often the safest place to hide from God."[4] What does he mean? I interpret his comment in this way: in our religious life, where our beliefs and practices inform our daily lives, we can perform, think, believe, and do things for God without truly knowing God's heart.

Judas Iscariot is a great example of this. He was one of the twelve disciples Jesus handpicked after praying through the night. He was also the money keeper for Jesus and part of the group Jesus sent out in pairs to preach or "tell the story," cast out demons, and perform miracles. Judas had a significant position of religious leadership, walked at Jesus's side during the Lord's entire public life of ministry—and did not truly know God intimately. One of the most profound glimpses at

Judas's soul, and an example of how religion can be a place to hide from God, is recorded in the Gospel of Matthew:

> When it was evening, [Jesus] reclined at table with the twelve. And as they were eating, he said, "Truly, I say to you, one of you will betray me." And they were very sorrowful and began to say to him one after another, "Is it I, Lord?" He answered, "He who has dipped his hand in the dish with me will betray me." (26:20–23)

The passage goes on to say, "Judas, who would betray him, answered, 'Is it I, *Rabbi*?'" (v. 25, emphasis added). Judas allowed Jesus partial access into his heart. That place of being authentically vulnerable before God never arrived for Judas. Jesus was his *rabbi*, not his *Lord*. Rabbi means "teacher." Jesus should be our teacher. His voice should inform how we live and what we believe. Scripture is clear, however, that every knee will bow and every tongue confess—not that Jesus is Rabbi, but Lord (see Phil. 2:10–11). It would have served Judas well to slow down, pay attention to the condition of his soul, and notice how far he truly was from his inheritance. Judas never fully stepped into the story he became so familiar with.

Losing God in Religion

I am going to suggest something a bit provocative that requires an intentional pause on our part: we can be more committed to Christianity than we are to Jesus. We can be more committed to the story about God and, over time, like the idea of God more than we do God as a Person. Jesus did not come to the earth to merely create a religion called Christianity. His body was not marred beyond the form of human likeness so we could have a "Jesus-branded life." Jesus did not come because he is the most relevant way or the most popular way. Jesus is not the cool way. He is not the American way. Jesus himself declared he is "the [only] way, and the truth, and the life" (John 14:6).

Life with God means there is always much, much more. God is worthy of your relentless pursuit. If you realize that, maybe, there are some parts of your heart that are not fully yielded to God, don't be ashamed. God is inviting you to come closer. It takes courage to refuse to use God's sovereignty and unconditional love as an excuse to settle. You can finally pursue God with everything you are. Has a piece of your soul lagged behind? Are you longing for more of God and the fulfillment of what God promised to you in Scripture? Perhaps you have hit a wall in prayer and, rather than finding God in the silence, you quit praying altogether. Now, you realize you have succumbed to what may be the ultimate form of pride: prayerlessness. Or you started out in your relationship with God with deep conviction and somewhere along the way, possibly, Jesus became just another rabbi. Slowly but surely, maybe you or someone you love started making decisions to live life with the Christian label on it, but the substance of God's presence has begun to fade.

We pray the same familiar prayer every time before we eat and fail to truly recognize how special the food we have in front of us is. I have done that. We peruse social media during church, if we are even in the rhythm of attending, because we have "heard all there is to know about John 3:16 before." Sometimes people justify subtle compromises because they believe everything they think and feel, even if it does not line up with Scripture, is correct.

I know what it is like to try to win the argument when humility was the better way. I have chosen anxiety when, within my heart, I heard the words of Jesus from Scripture resound to "not be anxious about tomorrow" (Matt. 6:34). I have been so used to my anger and emotional dysfunction that I didn't know how to live without it. All while sitting casually with my coffee, numbly reading over words like, "her sins, which are many, are forgiven—for she loved much. But he who is forgiven little, loves little" (Luke 7:47). I told people I would pray for them and then walked away and forgot. In these things, and many more, I found a perfect hiding place from God in religion. This is not a new phenomenon—and it is certainly not one we should accept.

In Ezekiel 10:15–19, Scripture says the glory of the Lord departed from the temple. For decades following, before the temple was destroyed by the Babylonians, Israel and its priests continued to perform hollow religious traditions when the object of their affection and worship was long gone. It's almost as if they sat at God's table, like those in Revelation 3:20, and were surprised when a knock at the door came. We have no record anyone noticed. Sometimes you and I haven't noticed either. Now is a good time to start.

When you set out on your sacred chase, you are introduced to the reality of Jesus in your everyday life. Just like Jesus raised Lazarus from the dead, he can bring life to any situation that is lifeless. The same Jesus who fed the multitude with five loaves of bread and two small fish is able and willing to provide for your big and small needs. The same Jesus who extended grace by forgiving the woman caught in adultery also revealed grace by telling the religious leaders the truth of who they were and who they could become. He extends that same grace to you now. God's grace empowers you to live the reality of heaven day after day rather than providing an excuse to settle for less than God promised. Jesus is your new normal.

Let's Gogh

My favorite painting in the world is called "Starry Night." It was painted by Vincent van Gogh in June 1889, and it captures the view toward the east of Saint-Remy-de-Provence. Though he painted the view from his room in the asylum twenty-one times, none of the paintings he created include the bars across his window. Though today it is arguably his most well-known painting, when writing to his brother, van Gogh described it as a failure.[5] The painting is full of dark blue hues and bursts of goldenrod. The village in van Gogh's painting was added by the artist. For years I saw this painting in a variety of ways and, honestly, thought it was a bit ridiculous. It seemed like a picture of just another village nestled into some mountains. There was nothing of the painting that caused me to say, "That's my favorite piece of art in the world"—that is, until I learned the story behind it.

Vincent van Gogh, a genius who spoke five languages and wrote fluently in three, is known in the history books as a mentally insane artist who severed his own ear and later took his life. The fact that he wrestled with his internal and external realities is heartbreaking. He struggled with life, happiness, injustice, and also Christianity. Born into a lineage of Dutch Reformed pastors, he himself was trained to follow suit. After he was rejected to serve in vocational pastoral ministry by denominational leaders, he began working and living with the poor in the tradition of the Franciscans. His willingness to live in the worst conditions so he could love the forgotten ones offended church authorities, and he was "pronounced unfit for the dignity of the priesthood."[6]

Though not formally trained as a painter, he found art was a more effective medium than a pulpit was to communicate his deep feeling of compassion for the suffering and how he felt God's presence among them. For the majority of his life, he seemed to vacillate between religious devotion and religious rejection. During one of his seasons of religious devotion, he even sought to become a missionary, while announcing later in life that "the God of the clergymen, he is for me as dead as a doornail."[7] Later he called himself "no friend of present-day Christianity." His struggle was less with the teachings of Jesus and much more with the corrupt institutional church of his day. Studying van Gogh's writings and paintings reveals how a soul can struggle to bring what one knows to be true about God together with one's life experiences.

It was during a time of religious devotion, as mental illness became increasingly real to him, that his most celebrated work, known as "Starry Night," emerged. It is a visual parable. The scene is of a small village or hamlet underneath a sky filled with turmoil. Deep indigo represents the infiniteness of God's presence, and streams and bursts of yellow symbolize sacred love. They are undeniably strong in the artist's work. The yellow stars in the sky illuminate the homes in the small village. In his commencement address at Biola University in May 2012, artist Makoto Fujimura explained, "The cypress tree and the church are two forms that connect heaven and earth."[8] For the artist, heaven and earth shared the same reality. The buildings in the imaginary town under the stars near Saint-Remy all emanated the same light—all but one. The church.

It appears the artist did not see a true representation of God in the religious system of his day. The church building he painted resembles those in his native Holland, not France.⁹ He said, "When I have a terrible need of—shall I say the word—religion, then I go out and paint the stars."¹⁰

When it came to his experiences with religion, whether it is because he didn't fit a specific mold the church of his day was looking for or perhaps because he struggled to know who he truly was in Christ, van Gogh seemed to hit a brick wall. His experience reveals that those who have been wounded in the name of religion and church often struggle to find God there. For us all, van Gogh serves as a reminder that there is no reason why we should allow those wounds to distract us from our pursuit of God.

I am thankful God is creating a community of all ages and all ethnicities, of members of society both rich and poor, of the famous and the unknown, called the church. There is immense value when we organize our traditions, beliefs, and symbols to pass them down to the generations to come. As in the case of Judas Iscariot, religion can be a good thing or a bad thing, depending on the condition of the human heart.

When I talk about the sacred chase, I am not saying that Jesus Christ himself should become an adjective to you. I am not asking you to be a Christian teacher, a Christian parent, or a Christian artist. I am saying Jesus invites you in this moment to experience the reality of every single one of God's promises in your life. For that reality to occur, it isn't just up to God; it is up to you too. We must all uniquely and individually own where our story began and, more importantly, what it will become with God. There is no limit on your connection with God unless you choose to put one there.

I like the way the Passion Translation puts Psalm 63:8: "With passion I pursue and cling to you. Because I feel your grip on my life, I keep my soul close to your heart." This verse refers to the psalmist making a commitment to follow, chase, and pursue God at whatever pace God decides to lead. And our soul is the key to following God closely and intimately.

CHAPTER THREE

God Welcomes You . . .
Wherever You Are

The vulture's eyes were not the only set watching the little Sudanese girl.

The bird stood there glaring at her. God designed her to be someone's little princess. I wonder if anyone ever told her that. She was on her way to the feeding station underneath the scorching African sun with drought-ridden land underneath her bare feet. Her decrepit physical condition was appalling to see. Her body was dehydrated and provided no perspiration to cool down her body temperature. The heat had baked her skin and dried it like a tanner would leather. Some would say she was one of the lucky ones, for she had made it that far. Somehow, she'd sojourned from her village, on a barren riverbed, to fight her way yet again to partake of an ancient human right—food—that still so many are denied. Corporate greed, corrupt political ideologies, or individualism still reign in parts of the world and leave beautiful people and amazing stories unknown and untold, and millions of us are simply unaware.

How could this little girl's beautiful story, handwritten by God for her life, be unrealized? It didn't seem right. It isn't right. And photographer Kevin Carter asked himself a similar question when he became aware and decided to do something about it.

Kevin was born in 1960 in Johannesburg, South Africa.[1] The same year Nelson Mandela's African National Congress was outlawed, Kevin entered a home where apartheid was accepted. But even at a young age, he despised apartheid's injustice. Like most of the South African young men in his generation, Kevin entered the South African Defense Force to serve and protect his national regime. Once his term ended, he wandered into a camera shop and began working there to put some money in his pocket. And the seed for photojournalism was planted within him.

He soon was making decent money as a weekend sports photographer. The money, though, wasn't enough for Kevin. The deep sense of justice he had even as a child, often speaking out against apartheid and poverty, emerged with a strong voice when he became an adult. He soon exchanged the loud crowds at sporting events to take photos that could help bring an end to the cries of the hurting. His camera became a lens through which the world saw injustice. His life's purpose was to expose humanitarian devastation, and he risked his life numerous times doing so. Kevin made sacrifices few human beings do. He was arrested several times and even placed himself in the line of fire, and Kevin's ability to tell the story of humanity's evil side, in hope that the good side would awaken, caught the attention of journalists around the world.

In 1993, Kevin left the violent, polarized culture in South Africa and traveled north to Sudan. It was there, as he walked across the barren ground that crackled underneath his feet like popcorn, that he saw the vulture. The bird's eyes seemed to have a focus that, if possessed by the good side of humanity, could end the suffering Kevin sought to eradicate through storytelling. Kevin wanted to expose poverty and injustice, not out of exploitation but in hope that soon a better day for the vulnerable around the world would come. Like Samuel the prophet in David's story, Kevin's camera was the prophetic voice knocking on the door of the modern world.

Too often, the pain of this world becomes too much for us to bear, and we justify it—or worse, hide it. Philip Berrigan, who told the stories of injustice he personally experienced as an activist, put it this way: "The poor tell us who we are, and the prophets who we should be. So, we hide the poor and kill the prophets."[2]

And the vulture stood there, waiting.

For twenty minutes Kevin waited and watched as the precious, malnourished girl crawled, walked, and collapsed again on her way toward the feeding station. Twenty minutes is a long time for the perfect photo to emerge. Kevin was thirsty. The girl was literally starving to death. The air was dry and arid. Sweat beaded up and dripped down Kevin's face. He must have felt empty. His passionate determination to tell one more story was all he had left.

A mere second is all it takes for the light, the lens, and chemical process to work once a photographer pushes a simple button. And at last, the second came.

After the girl's story was forever captured for the world, Kevin immediately charged toward the bird in an effort to send it away from the girl. She propped herself up again and continued her sojourn to survive, one short but long step at a time, toward the small station where a bowl of food and a drink awaited her.

Kevin recounted to an interviewer how this was a significant tipping point for him.[3] He set down his gear underneath a tree and just melted. He lit a cigarette and wept, and he talked to God that day. It is in moments like this that authentic prayer happens, away from the choirs and rehearsed religious dialect where people can often merely perform. I don't know anything about Kevin's spiritual life. I do know that the fact God experienced pain when Jesus of Nazareth died is evidence that there are some things God is not responsible for, that God doesn't prevent, and that God fully understands.

The *New York Times* purchased Kevin's picture of the little girl with the vulture on March 26, 1993. On April 12, 1994, the young girl's story was shared with the world, and the coveted Pulitzer Prize was awarded to Kevin for his work.

I do not know what happened to that beautiful girl, whose heart was just as full of dreams as any other, but her situation and her world kept them imprisoned. She is one of the unnamed ones. I pray she is never one of the forgotten ones. We do, however, know what happened to Kevin. A passionate human being, devoted to telling the stories that matter in a world filled with temporary pleasures, like bigger homes and nicer things, which too often are better brands of misery and the illusion of constant progress, he did not escape his demons. They traveled with him. He had wrestled underneath that tree, the smoke from the cigarette rising across his face, wondering *why*. I doubt receiving an award as relished and prized as the Pulitzer was worth the twenty minutes of torment he endured to create that photographic symbol of injustice.

His suicide note revealed the torment he endured and the grip of his memories. He admitted, "I am haunted by the vivid memories of killings and corpses and anger and pain . . . of starving or wounded children, of trigger happy madmen, often police, of killer executioners."[4]

What Lies Within

Kevin's documentation of the humanitarian crisis in Sudan raised awareness, people were moved to action, and lives were saved. Kevin was far from apathetic. He took what he believed and did something with it. You may not struggle with spiritual apathy nor have difficulty applying what you believe. You may, however, need greater understanding of who you are deep down inside. Kevin became aware of the injustice and evil affecting millions just like that little girl and was moved to action. But somewhere along the line he was no longer aware the pain in his own soul could have been healed. Awareness is a powerful thing.

His tragic death reveals a fundamental flaw in the human condition that can affect us all: we can fail to care for our own soul even when we care for others or outwardly appear successful. Coming to God, through Christ, and accepting the free gift of salvation is no different. When we do so we can also forget to care for our soul. It doesn't take long for this reality to emerge.

Third John 2 says, "I pray that all may go well with you and that you may be in good health, as it goes well with your soul." The condition of our soul will literally influence the way we view God, our life, our past, and our current reality; how we interpret Scripture; and the shape of our future. It feels dangerous to become vulnerable and deal with what's there. But this isn't nearly as dangerous as ignoring it or pretending it isn't there. Either our previous experiences will shape the expectations we have of our future or God's character and audacious love for us will. Awareness of our soul's condition provides clues as to where to begin setting aside those things that get in the way of our sacred chase, like Hebrews 12:1–2 talks about.

Adam and Eve had never sinned and they were still deceived. Why? They lacked awareness of what was going on deep within.

When God Breathed

Ancient Hebrew Scripture records in Genesis 1:1–5 that God spoke and the universe began. Genesis 2:7 says, "Then the LORD God formed the man of dust from the ground and breathed into his nostrils the breath of life, and the man became a living creature." Literally, the man became "a soul." Rabbinical scholars teach that the dust God formed the man from came from either all four corners of the earth or from what would be the future site of the altar of the temple. Though the reasons for both are not relevant for this book, I came across an interpretation of this that was fascinating. Many rabbis believe these two interpretations point toward two attributes of the condition of our soul: we have a yearning to understand the world beyond and a yearning for our home and roots.[5] In essence, there is a deep longing for what lies just beyond to come close.

Deep down, the human heart longs for an authentic connection with God, and often we just don't seem to know how to proceed. Many of you reading this book have prayed and "committed your life to Christ" but still find areas in your life absent of the divine breath. You may not feel seen, heard, or known by God. You know some information and have some beliefs, but you still long for more. Longing for more is all right. You were intentionally designed this way.

Your soul stretches far beyond who people perceive you to be and who you pretend to be. Beyond the veneer of religious performance, who you are eventually surfaces, and when that happens it can often be the most painful experience in your life. But for those courageous enough to be authentic with God, it can be the most liberating experience to realize how God sees us. God knows the condition of our soul and still chose to give us his Son. Why? We belong with him. This is our true identity, purpose, and eternal hope. But for some reason, though we trust God with our eternal destination after we die, it is easy and convenient to tolerate the baggage and issues traveling with us in life. Maybe we believe God's grace ignores them, or we think we are simply destined to live with them.

I am not talking about self-condemnation. Brené Brown says, "Shame damages the roots from which love grows."[6] We can go down a deep hole spiritually if we consistently go looking for things wrong in our lives. For those in Christ there is no condemnation, and each one of us is more than a conqueror (Rom. 8). I am also not talking about using God's grace as an excuse to tolerate spiritual poison. Someone I deeply esteem and personally respect is Bill Johnson, the senior leader of Bethel Church in Redding, California. One time I heard him say, "If grace does not lead you to holiness it is no grace at all."

What I'm suggesting is that we must never use relevance as an excuse to compromise. For those who live a Christian lifestyle but like Judas are far from God's heart, you may need a reminder that adjusting your lifestyle is not equal to walking humbly and purely before God. There is a realm of intimacy with God based solely on the access to your heart you provide to God. Self-awareness can be difficult. We know the areas we fall short—and yes, we all have them. If you're reading this book, it is highly likely you see some area in your life you want to grow in, produce change in, and humble yourself in. God is not mad at you. God loves you. Let God see what he already sees, deep down inside of you.

There is a perspective found in the eyes of Jesus alone. When you look closely, you see a true reflection of who you are and were created to be. You also catch a glimpse of any baggage in your soul lurking near. I often hear pastors and Christians say, "God wants to make us look more like Jesus." I understand what they mean. I agree. We are to be conformed to his likeness. An unintended consequence of a statement like this, however, is that it can make us forget that God's ultimate goal is not for us to become identical robots. We are made in God's image, and ultimately God wants us to become more like who we were created to be. Why? In Christ, we are found in him (Col. 3:3). There is an expression of Jesus that the world will never see if you are not authentically you. Trading the world's expectation of who you should be with who God formed you to become is not comfortable or easy. It is dangerous. But whoever said Jesus was safe and mediocre?

The mere mention of mediocrity and Jesus in the same sentence is an anomaly to me. Jesus was far from mediocre. Dorothy Sayers puts it this way:

The people who hanged Christ never, to do them justice, accused him of being a bore. On the contrary, they thought him too dynamic to be safe. It has been left for later generations to muffle up that shattering personality and surround him with an atmosphere of tedium. We have very efficiently pared the claws of the Lion of Judah, certified him "meek and mild," and recommended him as a fitting household pet for pale curates and pious old ladies.[7]

The Lion of Judah is not a kitten. He is not a pet. Jesus is actively involved in your life, and he lovingly invites you to do the hard, painful work of confronting who you currently are and begin moving toward who you were created to be.

Did I just use the words *confronting* and *Jesus* in the same thought? Yes, I did. Confrontation is not the same as conflict. Sometimes we need to confront ourselves and pastor our heart to move from where we are to where God invites us to be.

Let's Get Real

We become discouraged when our religious experience does not line up with God's good heart. Lacking identity, we develop a version of who we pretend to be, and we put on a show at work, in front of our spouse, at the gym, on the golf course, at church, or in the coffee shop. We are just terrified that people won't like who we really are. In our pretension, we can even forget the truth ourselves. We can perform for the approval of others until we are unaware it is a performance.

When life doesn't go as planned, our health is up in the air, those we love are making poor decisions, or we need direction, it is too easy to blame God in a passive-aggressive way and call it prayer. Though it breaks my heart to say this, some of you reading this are steeped in pornography and are used to fake intimacy. It doesn't bother you like it used to. You lack self-awareness.

Or perhaps your prescription from the doctor was more than you needed. You started taking some of the pills to sleep at night although your infection and symptoms were gone. This has been going on for weeks. You justify it because it's legal—though self-medication is often unwise.

Or you are arguing with your spouse and the phone rings. Instantly you are able to calmly answer it, and now your soul thinks that is normal. Are you aware of your soul's condition?

Has your time praying, reading Scripture, and simply being with Jesus remained constant?

Do you tolerate in your family the very things that destroyed your childhood?

Our disappointments in relationships can make building a wall to keep people out our first response. We can judge and criticize those we understand the least and even adopt religious language as a means to justify it. We can volunteer at church and not even know God. We can stop going to church because we assume everyone there is fake. We worry about our children because we begin to see in them the very things we wanted desperately to cure in ourselves before they were passed on.

The convenience of excuse invites the slow death of compromise into our lives.

The fear of being ordinary fuels our justification to do whatever it takes to get ahead.

When God points things out in our lives through the Holy Spirit, it is not to discourage us or punish us; rather, it is an invitation to experience greater spiritual freedom and release. When God reveals those areas we fall short in, it is his way of saying, "Hey, I know you are so much better than this. I love you enough to tell you the truth. I also love you enough to help you through this." It is God's kindness that leads you, and me, to change (Rom. 2:4). This simple truth is often overlooked. Soul-awareness is a spiritual discipline, a gift, that opens up a never-ending discovery of God's love. Soul-awareness is a result of a conversation with the Holy Spirit who, 24/7, inter-acts with us and reveals who we are and who we are becoming (John 16:7–17).

The key is this: to understand that your true self is in Christ. Self-awareness apart from Christ will only lead to discourage-ment and feelings of inferiority. Knowing that you are in Christ (Col. 3:3) means you have biblical self-awareness, which is look-ing at yourself through the eyes of God. This is when your life really begins to experience significant, sustainable change. What you believe about yourself and God echoes throughout every chamber of your soul. It will reverberate in your marriage, family, vocation, community, and generation. Trust me: you want to make sure that echo is based on accuracy.

Soul Searching

We may look in the mirror and scarcely recognize who we've become. Jesus of Nazareth knew this tendency well when he spoke the words in Mark 8:36: "For what does it profit a man to gain the whole world and forfeit his soul?" The word "gain" is literally translated "win" in the Greek New Testament.[8] You and I can finish the race, and even appear to win it, but if our human soul remains left behind on the track, crying out, and we noticed it not, we lose. As I travel and speak, I meet countless—and I do mean countless—individuals who have a familiarity with the Bible, hold leadership positions, have a religious mindset or spiritual lifestyle, accomplish a few goals, attend church—and some by their own admission go through life with a barren, dry soul. Unfortunately, most of the time we don't even see it. I know I didn't in my own life.

George Orwell wrote in his journal,

> Reading Mr. Malcolm Muggeridge's brilliant and depressing book, "The Thirties," I thought of a rather cruel trick I once played on a wasp. He was sucking jam on my plate, and I cut him in half. He paid no attention, merely went on with his meal, while a tiny stream of jam tricked out of his oesophagus. Only when he tried to fly away did he grasp the dreadful thing that had happened to him. It is the same with modern man. The thing that has been cut away is his soul, and there was a period— twenty years, perhaps—during which he did not notice it.[9]

Have you noticed your soul slipping away?

Mark 8:36 should give us reason to pause. The Bible draws a clear distinction between our soul and spirit. The centuries of Bible translations and the various versions, though incredibly valuable, cause the modern-day reader to lose much of the original distinction between the terms. There are a few main words in the Greek New Testament that nuance this. To fully embrace all Jesus is saying in Mark 8:36, a few realities are important to understand. For starters, Jesus uses a particular word in this verse, *psuche*.

Psuche means "mind, will, and emotions," which is where we get our word *psychology*.[10] *Psuche* comes from a word meaning to "breathe or blow," and points toward each individual's unique identity. This is often synonymous with other words like *kardia*, which is translated "heart," and, you guessed it, serves as the root for our word *cardiology*.[11]

Pneuma means "spirit," and this is where we get our word *pneumatic*, for it means "forceful wind."[12] *Zoe* means "life,"[13] and this is what happened to the beggar in Acts 3: "And leaping up, he stood and began to walk, and entered the temple with them, walking and leaping and praising God" (v. 8). The former beggar was touched in his body for he *walked*, he was touched in his soul for he was *leaping*, and he was changed in his spirit for he *praised* God. Spirit, soul, and body should be impacted when we meet God. Hebrews 4:12 reminds us that Scripture is "piercing to the division of soul and of spirit," further reinforcing the importance of paying attention to our soul. Our soul and our spirit are two separate realities. We are never more alive in our bodies than when our spirit and soul experience renewal together.

When we become spiritually new (John 3:3), our spirit becomes alive in Christ. Our body remains the same. Our soul, however, is unique. We do not receive a brand-new soul when Jesus breathes life into us. Our soul is destined to experience a unique process of renewal—and this, my friend, is not just up to God; it is up to you and me.

Cowriting the Next Chapter with God

Remember, God gives the Spirit without measure and limit. We are invited to cowrite with him the next chapter in his story for our lives. Jesus paid the price for our eternal salvation, but our quality of life with God and our spiritual health are primarily up to each of us. This isn't always easy, and it requires effort on our part. Effort is not striving for perfection; rather, it is a deliberate posture of the heart that says, *God, I want to know you more, whatever the cost.*

God does not give us amnesia when we become Christians. We still must renew, or remodel, the old house of our soul, where all of our thoughts, memories, and emotions coexist. Romans 12:1–2 invites us to walk with God on a pilgrim's path toward renewal where, day after day, as we run toward the end, we slow down and listen to the bits and pieces of our soul that have fallen down on the track behind us.

The prophet Ezekiel described this when he saw a valley full of bones (Ezek. 37). Bones were often a metaphor in the Hebrew Bible for our soul and identity, and these were scattered abroad. As they assembled into a mighty army, they were nothing without the breath of God in them. The old bones needed to be renewed. James 5:8 puts it this way: "You also, be patient. Establish your hearts."

James tells us to *establish* our hearts, or literally, to plant them securely. It is possible to plant our heart in God so we flourish and bud even out of season. How do I know this? In Numbers 17, Aaron, the high priest, placed his rod in the presence of God, and even an inanimate dead stick bloomed and came alive again. How much more can the Lord do with someone remarkable, like you, formed in his very image?

When Jesus declares we can gain the entire world but forfeit our soul, he is not necessarily referring to eternal life. Jesus invites us to plant our soul in the presence of God just like Aaron's rod. Jesus is saying, in Mark 8:36, that we can try to finish and win the race and lose our *psuche*, our soul or the very breath within us, along the way. We are asked to be aware of what's going on within ourselves. In our walk with God, sometimes we win not by receiving first place but by slowing down and noticing if something just isn't quite right.

Why don't we slow down in our lives and do this? I'm convinced we lack understanding of who God really is, we don't think God is all that interested in us, we don't know what is truly accessible in our spiritual walk, or we simply don't know where or how to begin. Believe it or not, the sacred chase doesn't begin with us. It begins with God.

Running the Wrong Way

Some races are also won when the runners slow down.

One year before I was born, Seattle, Washington, hosted the 1976 Special Olympics. Parents, grandparents, guardians, foster parents, friends, and I'm sure plenty of press packed the stands to watch one of the smallest, more obscure races you can imagine. Well, it was obscure to the casual observer, but to those who'd traveled far and wide to run the 100-yard dash, this race was one of the biggest moments of their lives. We live in a world where speedy and charismatic athletes rule the day and bring with them plenty of lucrative sponsorships from the elite companies. No one speaks of your name after the race finishes unless you win gold or set a record. On this particular day, however, everyone in the stands learned an awful lot about what it means to truly win and how races are supposed to be run.

Hugs and kisses were heaped on the participants as each one, with their own story of struggle, support, and overcoming, meandered to the starting line. Some of the runners stood in amazement at the cheering fans while others bent their knees, focused on the track ahead, and waited for the starting gun to sound. The sound of the gun startled a few of the runners as each of the nine contestants began moving toward the finish line, trying their best to stay in their assigned lanes. The crowd went wild and the runners' names were heard from their loved ones.

"Come on, Jimmy!" "You can do it!" "Woohoo!"

All was well until one of the runners, a little boy, stumbled and fell to the ground. Those ahead continued to run toward the finish as he sat there, crying. Some of the crowd were concerned but not shocked. After all, each one of the runners had fallen a time or two in their lives and were accustomed to getting back up and continuing. Their participation in the Special Olympics was enough to prove that.

Two other runners in the race heard the little boy crying. They slowed down, took their eyes off of the finish line for just a moment, and glanced back to see what was going on. Those two runners did not vacillate for one moment. As soon as they both saw the little boy crying on the track, they turned around and ran back toward him.[14] Runners aren't supposed to run the opposite direction on a track. Runners aren't supposed to be more concerned about the safety and well-being of someone else when the gold medal is at stake. Everybody knows when you run a race, you run to win. But perhaps winning doesn't always mean getting the gold medal or first-place ribbon.

The little boy was helped up by the other two runners. Side by side, the three linked arms and walked down the track toward the prize. As they crossed the finish line, the fans stood to their feet, shouting and celebrating, crying and smiling, as they witnessed what true champions look like.

I catch a glimpse of God's love for us when I think of that Special Olympics race. When we fall down, God is right there to make sure we know that we don't run alone. Sometimes we just need to be reminded that God comes looking for us when we are having a hard time on our journey.

Some reading this simply *want* a greater connection with God because you love him so much. Others, possibly resonating with some of the examples I've provided, would admit to *needing* a greater connection to God. Whether you fall into the *want* or *need* category, God responds to you in the same way: *I have been waiting for you to give just one glance in my direction. Now that you have, let's chase the inheritance my Son Jesus died to provide you with.*

There was a man in Mark 5 whose name we do not know, but his spiritual condition is arguably one of the worst found in the Bible. His soul was almost completely gone. Against all odds, he overcame every excuse to be apathetic and courageously, in vulnerability, became aware of who God truly was. He began the sacred chase. God welcomed the one they called Legion when he started his pursuit. Regardless of how much of the world you have gained or lost, God welcomes you in your pursuit of him too.

CHAPTER FOUR

Legion's Greatest Treasure

As a child I was fascinated with outer space. Due to the vastness of our universe, when we gaze into the sky at the flickering light of the stars, we are actually peering back in time. What do I mean? Light travels at approximately 186,000 miles per second, but since the universe is so large and is still expanding, some of the stars that we see shining have actually already burned out. It just takes a while for the darkness to replace the light, speeding through space, that is hitting the human eye. The wonders of God's creation are just too amazing. Job 5:9 captures it well: "[God] does great things and unsearchable, marvelous things without number."

Scientists recently caught a glimpse of one of the most violent and terrifying things to occur in the cosmos: the crash of two neutron stars. It showed up on their scientific instruments as a mere whisper. This crash happened while dinosaurs supposedly roamed the earth, but the signal had to travel 130 million light-years to reach us, and it arrived here in mid-August 2017.[1] This quiet signal caused astronomers all around the world to stop everything they were doing, aim telescopes placed on every continent around the world, and focus in on a distant spot somewhere "out there." More than four thousand scientists devoted themselves to studying the phenomenon.

When a star collapses, its core is so dense that a teaspoon of its matter would weigh 1 billion tons. When two of these cores, or neutron stars, collide, it causes something like a cosmic fireworks display. The crash generates gamma rays, a gravitational wave, and a ripple in space and time. I'm not sure what all of this means, but it gets real special in a moment: not only did this event produce an indescribable explosion but it also produced elements. Calculations revealed the resulting amount of heavy elements, such as gold, platinum, and uranium, are 1,300 times the mass of Earth.

Yes, the sky is literally full of gold.

Now, the last time I looked, there were around 13.6 million millionaires in the United States alone.[2] That is a staggering number to me. I remember as a child thinking a million dollars was unheard of and, frankly, it was where I came from. It seems more and more common in our age. When it comes to billionaires, there are around 2,200 worldwide.[3] Are there any trillionaires? The verdict is still out on when that will happen. How it will happen is another story.

Some economists believe the first trillionaire will emerge when outer space is commercialized. Where in the world do they get that idea? Cosmic gold hunters will one day try to harvest the remnants of explosions like the one we witnessed in 2017. Other near-Earth asteroids are also full of precious metals, like gold, that are waiting for someone to cash in what some say is a "twenty-trillion-dollar check."[4]

True Treasure

There are immeasurable, valuable treasures released in ways, like interstellar explosions that belong in a Marvel or Star Wars movie, we cannot fully understand. But just because we don't see the treasure doesn't mean it isn't there. There is another mind-blowing amount of treasure I want to tell you about as well. That treasure is God within you (2 Cor. 4:7–11). Galatians 2:20 says, "I have been crucified with Christ. It is no longer I who live, but Christ who lives in me."

Deuteronomy 7:6 says, "The LORD your God has chosen you to be a people for his treasured possession." This verse refers to God setting apart a group of people, called Israel, as his own. First Peter 2:9–10 shows us that, in Christ, this is now our identity as well. We are God's treasure. He loves us, not because of what we've done but because of who he is.

With this truth in mind, as we look at current reality in life, and all that went into bringing us here, sometimes what we think, feel, and experience leads us to a different conclusion. Rather than feeling treasured by God, sometimes we feel forgotten. This occurs when we allow our circumstances to dictate how we perceive God.

One of the main reasons people don't begin or continue the sacred chase of living a life devoted to discovering the love of God is because they feel God isn't there or isn't involved, or because they think God is not approachable. I believe much of this comes from a saying often heard when life gets hard. Whenever tragedy hits, someone will say, "Oh well; God has a purpose." Try telling that to the ones who were abused. To the children who grow up in poverty because of gambling debts. Did God really choose this to be his grand plan for their lives? Is

God sovereign? Yes. Is God a good Father? Yes. Tragedies occur that are not necessarily God's fault. When a drunk driver slams into another vehicle, altering everyone's life forever, God cannot be blamed for the one who got behind the wheel intoxicated. Sometimes things happen that have nothing to do with God's "purpose," but rather than dealing with the pain of life and being vulnerable with the God who also feels, we edit God's love out of our story with calloused "theological" sayings.

Romans 8:28 reminds us that in all things God works for our good. For whom? The Scripture says, "for those who are called according to *his* purpose" (emphasis added). Although God may not cause everything to happen day after day, like whether you'll choose to eat a cheeseburger or tacos for lunch, he is certainly with you right where you are. He actively partners with you in life (Eph. 1:11). He does this by introducing you to the real you.

Right now, regardless of your situation and experience, you are positioned and invited by God for a greater connection with him. The circumstances we would typically use as excuses to avoid the sacred chase actually serve as the delivery system for our divine invitation. What happens when spiritual passion and soul-awareness collide in the presence of Jesus? All of heaven's resources are released to propel you and me forward in our sacred chase. Just like the sky is full of priceless things, our life is also filled with divine promises—even when they can't be seen.

Winds, Waves, and the Wild Man

A familiar story to many of us is found in Mark 4:35–41, when Jesus calms the storm. In my Bible, the heading of this section is "Wind and Wave Obey Jesus." In another translation, the heading says "Jesus Calms the Storm." These headings are useful but they are not part of the original text. They are simply inserted for readability. This story, which is full of amazing truths, is about much more than Jesus calming a storm. I suggest it is about Jesus, who knew full well a storm would come, choosing to use the storm to deliver an invitation of God's unconditional love. To whom? To one of the most inspiring individuals in the Bible, one who set aside thousands of excuses and dared to go on the sacred chase. Listening to our excuses in life is easy; choosing to cultivate a deeper connection to God in the midst of their hollow tirade is transformative.

Jesus and his friends had been hanging around the Sea of Galilee for a few days when they got into a boat. The disciples, many of whom had lifelong fishing experience, wouldn't have thought twice about it. But then a serious storm broke, and those disciples, who had just witnessed Jesus perform miracle after miracle, began to panic. Those who had tangible proof of God's ability to do the miraculous doubted God's ability when the circumstances became challenging. Sound familiar? I've often wondered why Jesus, knowing a storm would come, asked his closest friends to get into the boat. Perhaps it is a reminder that not all of life's storms are a result of a scheme by our spiritual enemy to destroy us. Some storms come by divine invitation, and all of them are under the watchful eye of the One who can simply speak and calm them.

Where was God when the wind and waves threatened to tear the vessel to shreds while the disciples were terrified? Sleeping—in the bottom of the very boat the disciples were probably holding on to for dear life.

Jesus didn't stop the storm from starting but he did stop the storm from continuing. In a moment, the wind and waves were stilled. There are some storms God delivers us from and others God delivers us in. It is a miraculous story, just like we would expect when God is there.

The disciples were blown off course; they had left Capernaum for Bethesda only to wind up in a remote place in gentile territory called Gadara. I have a feeling, though, that the disciples may have been taken somewhere they never planned, but God knew all along where the boat would come to the shore: just in the right place for a wild, unsightly, and unusual person to greet them. This particular storm's purpose is recorded in Scripture for us all to see.

The storm on the Sea of Galilee (or Sea of Tiberias to the Romans) seemed to go on forever. The disciples panicked, terrified for their lives, and wondered where Jesus was. Why would God allow the storm to rage only to speak and immediately calm it later on? Sometimes God calms the storm immediately, and at other times God allows the wind and waves to continue to rage. Our response to God, however, should never be progressive, circumstantial, based on happenstance, or casual. Immediate obedience and immediate surrender are our only logical responses when Jesus is near.

Regardless of how you arrived where you are, God can use the storms of life—the "all things" of Romans 8:28—to introduce you to the next chapter of his story for you. Now is the time to set aside the excuses, the shame, the laziness, the apathy, the busyness, or even the good things life is often filled with to notice that the very One your heart longs to know has come to shore.

In the Gospel of Mark, something equally as miraculous as a storm being calmed was about to happen, and those closest to Jesus didn't know about it. That is usually the way it works when we allow life's distractions to become greater than the God who is with us.

The Man on a Chase

After the storm blew the boat off course, Jesus and his friends came ashore on the other side of the Sea of Galilee, to "the country of the Gerasenes" (Mark 5:1) or Gadara. Some translations and other Gospels say "Gergesenes" or "Gadarenes." In Semitic languages, "gader" means "wall or boundary," a reference potentially to the cliffs in the distance. According to Talmudic legend, supposedly this place is associated with the vineyard wall where an angel stopped the prophet Balaam (Num. 22:24–29).[5] But since the Greeks influenced this region significantly before the Roman Empire emerged, some believe it was called Gadara simply in memory of the Macedonian village of the same name.[6]

Though there is some debate among scholars as to exactly where the boat arrived ashore, due to these varying names, what is important to us is the fact that Jesus arrived at an unusual place, not on the "itinerary," because of the very storm the disciples would have preferred to avoid. Some of the most amazing moments with God occur like this. Life's storms can blow us to places we never imagined as we find ourselves, perfectly, within the reach of a loving God.

Perhaps their boat came aground with a grinding sound as its underbelly scraped along the shore, or perhaps they were able to tie up to a man-made dock, as modern archaeologists have found evidence in this location of significant boating. Either way, it didn't take a few hours or even a few days for the miracle to occur. Mark 5:2 says, "When Jesus had stepped out of the boat, immediately there met him out of the tombs a man with an unclean spirit." *Immediately*. It happened immediately. That is the power of one glance at Jesus; after all, he is where we find our greatest treasure. When you catch a glimpse of who God truly is, you don't have to think about it, consider it, or weigh the options.

Who was this man who ran (v. 6) immediately to Jesus? We don't know his name, but we do know how desperate he was. He was literally tormented by a multitude of evil spirits. When Jesus asked him his name, he replied, "My name is Legion, for we are many" (v. 9). *Legion* was a term used to describe a group of around six thousand Roman soldiers.[7] Some Bible scholars believe the man was Jewish due to the cultural nuances of his words.[8] Jesus was sent to the Jewish people at this time in his ministry, and the Gospels are clear when Jesus had contact with non-Jews.

To be clear, there are many mental and emotional challenges in life that do not involve demons. This is evident all over Scripture. Sometimes people need to talk through trauma, change their thought patterns, get their physical health under control, or consult a medical professional. There are times, however, when the condition of someone's spiritual life is so hopeless, he or she can literally be overwhelmed and captive by evil spirits. It is extremely important not to assume complete understanding of the spiritual world from one story in the Bible. We can learn, however, the nature of the unseen world, for it is much more real than anything we do see. This man was not just having a bad day, nor was he just struggling with some of life's issues. No, he was about as hopeless as someone could be; his life, literally, was almost completely controlled by evil spirits. He lived among the limestone caves that peppered the cliffs around the sea. Mark 5:3 calls these caves "tombs." Corpses were placed in them. Criminals and demonized individuals found safety in these supposedly haunted places. No one else dared to venture in.

As part of a region known as the Decapolis (meaning ten cities), Gadara offered a beautiful panoramic view of the surrounding countryside. Every day the one they called Legion arose from sporadic sleep to the light from the sunrise and stepped out of his cave. I imagine his astonishment at the stunning landscape and pink and orange hues from the sunrise in front of him would have been quickly dulled by his inner torment. You and I can also become numb to the beauty in our lives because of the darkness within. This is why Jesus said in Luke 11:35, "Therefore be careful lest the light in you be darkness." I wonder how often God surrounds us with opportunities, breakthroughs, miracles, and answers to prayer and we simply do not notice them because the eyes of our soul see dimly.

Gadara was not a remote fishing village in the middle of nowhere. It was a center for Greek culture and home to many well-known poets and philosophers such as Menippus.[9] But in a place where educational and philosophical advances were cutting edge and prosperity was attainable, this man was hopeless. The townspeople, afraid of him and the potential harm he might cause to their families, often bound him with chains (Mark 5:3). But in the man's tenacious torment and supernatural strength, he broke the chains and shackles in pieces. "No one had the strength to subdue him" (v. 4). *No one* (nothing, none) *had the strength* (to prevail, to have force) *to subdue* (to tame or restrain, to have force) *him*.[10]

This literal translation of Mark 5:4 provides a glimpse at the attitudes of those who tried to help the man and those who simply cast him aside. For some, the solution was to tame Legion. In other words, to try to get him to conform, pretend, mimic, or behave a certain way. Others forcefully chained him up to protect everyone from him, including himself. It is also possible some just wanted to cast him out of their region.

It is important not to see Legion as a man who was victimized by the choices of others who tried to tame him. It is likely those seeking to tame the man had his best interest at heart. Legion was hurting and a danger to society, and some around him were trying their best. The Christian life, however, is not one of taming people to conform. Followers of Christ do not memorize God; we become like him.

The man cried out night and day (v. 5). When it was light out, and people went about their busy lives, the one they called Legion screamed in torment. At night, when little children were being kissed good night and possibly prayed with in the pagan city, they were lulled to sleep by the familiar sounds of the one whose identity became the same as his condition. Scripture says the man also cut (a violent term meaning to hack) himself. As a self-mutilator, he would have been covered in dried blood, puss, scars, and scabs. Parts of his body may have even been self-amputated due to this self-imposed "hacking."

This individual, who lived with dead bodies, screamed night and day in torment, cut and hacked himself repeatedly, and wore no clothing (Luke 8:27), saw Jesus from afar and "ran and fell down before him" (Mark 5:6). What would you do if a naked, dirty individual covered in blood and scars came running straight for you, screaming and yelling at the top of his lungs? You would grab a Taser, a firearm, a bottle of pepper spray—or run for dear life. What did Jesus do? Jesus saw how vulnerable the man's quest for divine connection made him and simply asked the man what his name was. Why would Jesus want to know?

In the first century, when this moment took place, there was a belief in the Jewish religion that demons were individual, separate entities. For this reason, whenever someone came in contact with an evil spirit and its name was revealed, they cataloged it and maintained detailed lists.[11] This was one way they tried to learn how the unseen world worked. In my experience, the challenge with this is that evil spirits don't always tell the truth. Satan is the father of lies (John 8:44). In extreme cases of demonized individuals, it is never beneficial to talk with an evil spirit. Their speech is vulgar, untrustworthy, and a distraction from what really matters. But Jesus didn't ask the man his name for this reason.

There was also a belief that knowing the name of an evil spirit gave you special power over it.[12] But Jesus had all authority on the earth (Matt. 28:18) and didn't need to know the spirit's name to be effective in setting the man free. It is apparent that before he asked the man his name, Jesus commanded the demons to leave. Why they didn't leave immediately is a mystery to me, for they often did elsewhere. This is the only time in the New Testament when Jesus appears to have an in-depth conversation with evil spirits, but we are not given much detail or reason, and shouldn't assume what God has not deemed necessary to share with us. The reason is obviously not important to God; therefore, it isn't important to me. What is important is understanding why Jesus asked the man's name—and it wasn't so Jesus could have authority over him.

Apparently, Jesus addressed the evil spirits as the man was running toward him and, when the naked, bloody, hopeless man came close, Jesus spoke to the man. The issue of identity comes to the surface. I believe Jesus, in asking the man's name, was trying to remind the man that God still saw, beyond his struggle, a special person. Jesus humanized someone who felt untouchable.

Somehow, perhaps from the higher ground where the caves were, the man saw Jesus come to shore, and his immediate response was unbelievable. What did the man they called Legion see? If he believed God wasn't interested in him as a person, or that God would be embarrassed to be associated with him, he overcame that internal dialogue. If he believed Jesus would scold him and heap divine shame on him, he somehow overcame that thought as well. I believe even one small glance at Jesus reveals how loving and gracious God is. That one glance propelled the man to begin his sacred chase.

I saw Ali, my wife, for the first time in sixth grade. She doesn't remember it, but I do! We were in Mrs. Alexander's science class. I wrote her name down in a little notebook because I thought she was beautiful. I used to sneak peaks at her throughout the day. She was just perfect. In eighth grade, when we became "sweethearts," I used to ask the teacher for a bathroom pass so I could walk past Ali's classroom and look at her. From time to time I tried talking to her underneath the classroom door, oblivious to the reality that everyone in the classroom could hear me. We have been married for over twenty years now, and I still like to sneak peaks and catch another glance at her. When she sits at our dining room table with her latte and Bibles, I look at her. When we are on the couch with our girls watching a movie, I'll catch another glimpse. Driving down the road is another perfect opportunity to do so. With one glance at the love of my life, all of our history, memories, and the millions of reasons I love her collide. All it takes is one look, and she has my heart all over again. In *Les Miserables*, Victor Hugo said of a glance, "It is in this way that love begins, and in this way only."[13]

When we see who Jesus really is, no matter how many excuses or distractions we may have, everything within us gravitates toward him. For those who do not pursue Jesus this way, it is worth asking whether or not they have ever truly caught a glimpse of who God really is.

The man saw something approachable, down-to-earth, and accepting when he saw Jesus. Like we know the treasure in outer space exists, though we can't see from Earth, the man knew the priceless treasure of God's love was there. Even if his eye couldn't see it, his heart did. This man was so desperate to meet Jesus that he did not use his situation as an excuse to avoid chasing God. If this man could overcome all of the pain, torment, confusion, shame, and sheer desperation and run the sacred path to Jesus, surely you and I can as well. God came toward Legion, but the sacred chase was Legion's response to God's pursuit of him. Jesus came to the shore, but the man still had to come toward Jesus.

If you aren't sure where to start your wholehearted pursuit of Jesus, like Legion, just start right where you are by being open with God about how you feel.

Legion had a multitude of reasons to avoid being vulnerable before God, reasons why God wouldn't accept him because of his condition, and reasons why he wasn't cut out for the chase. When Jesus comes your direction, regardless of how unconventional the circumstance is, your soul's cry for more of God has greater intensity and influence than the sway thousands of demons held in Legion. When the human soul longs for Jesus, it cannot be held back even when thousands of voices tell us otherwise. God went through great lengths to close the gap between you and him by sending his Son, Jesus of Nazareth, into the world. The treasure of heaven was killed on the cross for you. Jesus died for a treasure fit only for the King of the universe. Jesus died for you.

A Truckload of Love

By the time the first responders arrived that April evening in 2018, it was approximately 1:00 a.m.[14] In northern Detroit on Interstate 696, some people were traveling to a diner for steak and eggs after working the evening shift. I'm sure a family or two had taken a few extra days for vacation and were headed home. Students were on their way back to their dorms to get ready for the summer break. And thirteen semitruck drivers were about to witness something they had never seen and, more than likely, never would again.

A man stood on the edge of an overpass, contemplating whether or not life was worth living. The first responders were quickly joined by additional police and rescue workers. Tragedy could strike in only a few moments, and the negotiators worked quickly but cautiously to talk the man away from the edge. Following usual protocol, all lanes of the highway under the bridge were also shut down. The police did not allow anyone in or out. But somehow, as the heroes tried desperately to prevent this man from committing suicide, something slipped through the barricade and ended up directly beneath the overpass.

Was it a small, obscure rabbit that made its way past security? Was it a smooth, stealthy runner who wanted to get a closer look at what was going on? Did someone fly a drone under the trees to gather footage? No, it was a semitruck, and its driver who just happened to be in the right place at the right time. You know, the huge, noisy, boisterous trucks on the highway? Yeah, somehow one of those just happened to creep in. But that was only the beginning.

Within a matter of moments, another truck joined, followed by a third and then a fourth. In total, thirteen rigs pulled underneath the bridge and formed a shield to shorten the drop from a potentially fatal distance to just a few feet should the desperate man choose to jump. As onlookers began to videotape what was happening, behind the scenes the Michigan State Police were organizing the truck drivers to assist. There were no educational prerequisites for the participants. Their gender or ethnicity was not a factor. Their age was not a concern. All that was necessary was a simple yes. The police later stated they were surprised to see so many drivers volunteer.

The man stood on the ledge while, for over three hours, negotiators stood on his left and right while semitrucks gathered below. Each time the man looked down, he would have been reminded that in such a large and often lonely world, he was noticed and cared for by those who knew him not. Surrounding this man by a multitude of people who desperately wanted him to make the right choice paid off. The man eventually stepped back from the edge and went to a hospital. The drivers, all who had somewhere to be—a load to deliver, possibly kids to greet just in time before heading off to school—drove off.

It wasn't convenient to slow down. They didn't get paid extra money to do so. They slowed down because they were invited to.

When extreme efforts are made to save someone, that person is shown they are worth much more than they originally thought. The drivers and first responders worked tirelessly and refused to give up on the man. In sending his Son, God went through immeasurably more to make sure we could be saved from our sins and thrive abundantly in this world. His life, death, and resurrection were to secure your salvation through faith in Christ.

Remember, salvation is like a door, and once you walk through it, you will discover the endlessness of God's promises and the immeasurability of your spiritual inheritance in Christ, and you will begin to know the love of God that is unknowable.

You have been invited by God into a never-ending, awe-inspiring, wondrous, amazing, supernatural pursuit. And like the man on the bridge, all that is needed from you is to say a simple yes to the display of love right in front of you. Don't confuse simple with easy. Simple doesn't always mean convenient. Simple certainly isn't mediocre or average. Simple merely means it isn't complicated, hard to obtain, or out of your reach.

Your simple yes to begin the chase after God's heart, which is sure to soak every area of your life with the reality of heaven's promises, can unlock a torrent of God's presence that will cause every seed buried deep within the soil of your heart to bloom and produce fruit. But each seed will remain dormant until you say your simple yet profound yes to pursue God with all you are.

CHAPTER FIVE

You Travel Not Alone

S ir Nicholas Winton was in the television studio among what
seemed to be a typical audience.[1] When he'd taken his seat,
he'd greeted a few strangers. But he was in the presence of
someone significant, and he didn't know it. Actually, there were
two dozen significant people in the studio audience with him,
and they knew exactly who he was. Winton's relationship to
those strangers before him started with the simple discovery
of a scrapbook in an attic years before.

Winton was born in May 1909 to German-Jewish parents
who raised their three children in a twenty-room mansion in
London. As a boy, he excelled in various activities such as fenc-
ing and education. After being apprenticed in international
banking, he worked in Hamburg, Berlin, and Paris. He returned
to London in 1931 to further his career as a stockbroker. He
served as an officer in the Royal Air Force and raised awareness and funds for charities. This heart for people was recognized when he was made a member of the Order of the British

Empire. But what many believe to be his most notable achievement remained hidden in plain sight for decades.

In 1988, his wife, a Dane named Grete, found a simple scrapbook filled with pictures, letters from strangers, various travel papers, and other notes in the attic one day. As it appeared to be somewhat meaningful, she probed her husband, who, after a casual and generalized response, instructed her to throw away the items. But she did not do so.

In the documents and papers were clues to hundreds of Jewish children whose lives had been rescued from the Nazis—by Winton's efforts. Grete began researching, and then she contacted a Holocaust historian. The full story soon began to emerge.

Upon a friend's request, in 1938 Winton had canceled a skiing trip and instead flew to Prague to assist in some humanitarian work with Jewish refugees. What he saw shocked him. There were large camps filled with people living in decrepit and horrendous conditions. Many of them were children, and immigration restrictions made escape seem impossible.

In what seems to be lifted from the script of a Hollywood film, Winton became involved in a massive rescue attempt that began after he saw the suffering in the camps. Britain had formed the Refugee Children's Movement, which helped ten thousand Jewish children in Germany and Austria flee to Britain before the war began, but there was no such program in Czechoslovakia—until Winton started one. He was stalked by Nazi agents, issued bribes, risked his life countless times, forged signatures, handled large sums of money, and met parent after parent to try to get their children safely away to a foreign land before the seemingly inevitable occurred.

Eventually the organization had to open a storefront to accommodate the number of desperate parents, but the long lines that formed outside of it made the German secret police take notice, and Winton was out of time. Of the five thousand children whom he had information on, only nine hundred were fully registered for the detailed rescue plan, which included lining up volunteer foster families in Britain to receive each one.

Back in Britain, as families volunteered to take the children, money was also raised, but the funds ran short. Winton used his own resources to continue the mission.

The war officially broke out only a few months after Winton's urgent response to save the children. He made bribes and forged transit permits that would allow the children to leave Czechoslovakia. One roadblock after another didn't keep Winton from persevering.

Just a few hours before Hitler syphoned off some of Czechoslovakia's provinces, increasing his stranglehold on the desperate country, children began boarding trains as parents forced them, often against their will, to go with strangers to an unknown place. A total of nine trains were loaded to transport the nine hundred children out of the grip of the murderous Nazis and to the sea, where they crossed to Harwich and eventually landed by train in London. It is there the Jewish children, each carrying a small bag and wearing a name tag, were greeted by welcoming children and parents who would become their new families.

Of the nine trains dispatched, eight made it through. One of them, carrying about 250 children on September 1, 1939, the same day Hitler invaded Poland, never made it out, and the children on the train were never seen again. The borders were closed. Any additional efforts to save more children by Winton and his colleagues had to cease. In the end, 669 children were saved because of Winton's efforts.

The heroism of this man was stashed away for decades in a little scrapbook in an attic. For fifty years, this story was forgotten by most of the world—with the exception of those who became known as "Winton's children." When the public began to take notice, the Wintons were invited to be part of a BBC television program called *That's Life.*[2]

The host asked audience members to stand if they had been helped by Winton, and dozens did. The video footage reveals the emotion, joy, and power of compassion that endured for generations because of Winton's efforts. He was surrounded by dozens of children—now parents and grandparents—who had survived because of him. Why did he do it?

When someone asked him that very question, he simply responded, "Some people revel in taking risks, and some go through life taking no risks at all."[3] Why didn't he ever tell his wife, whom he met after the war, even after all those years? It is apparent he thought what he did, though significant and life-changing for many, was just the normal thing to do.

I pray the world would be filled with people who, like Sir Nicholas Winton, live day after day doing what is right, honorable, courageous, and godly as if it were normal. It certainly should be.

Getting Used to Normal

Our world is a better place because some things have become "normal," as in the case of Winton. Our world, and our individual lives, can also suffer and fall short of God's great promises when what is inferior, unhealthy, dysfunctional, and ungodly becomes "normal." The devil does an amazing work behind the camouflage of normal. What we tolerate, we provide space for, and, like an incurable disease, it will wreak havoc on our very souls if we are not careful. Apathy and lack of soul-awareness can distract us. How? They convince us that our experience is as good as it will get. We settle and slow down or even stop our pursuit of God's reality in our lives. When we tolerate such inferior ways of living, we adapt to a new normal. What we think is balance can actually be a slow, spiritual fade.

To live a life soaked with heaven, the counterfeits of God's promise need to go.

Legion's condition was an accumulation of words spoken over him, experiences, choices he and others made, memories, and thoughts. It began with something often undetected, small, toxic, and disguised as normal. And believe it or not, the same is true for you and me as well. The condition of our soul—not who we pretend to be or who others perceive us to be but who we really are—determines whether we begin and finish our race.

The sacred chase requires us to take what we believe, overcome apathy, and make the next courageous step. This may mean closing the door to sin, changing the way we think by seeing life through God's eyes, realigning our priorities, or making hard decisions. It means we pause and become self-aware of our need for more of heaven's reality in our lives here and now by paying attention to our soul. From a place of humility and honesty, we answer God when he asks, as he did the man at Gadara, what our name is. There is something else we must do as we set aside those things that hinder our spiritual journey: we acknowledge they are there.

Like the fallen runner in the Special Olympics, do you feel like obtaining the promise and crossing that finish line is out of reach? God comes to you now, not to criticize you but to help you continue. Does what you know to be true need to be put into practice, like Tilly Smith did on the shores of Mai Khao beach? Regardless of what people may think, this is your moment to act on what you believe.

Have you devoted yourself to success in the world's eyes only to find that, deep inside, something needs your attention? Have you tolerated anything in your life that unfortunately has become normal, and now you are beginning to see a downward spiral in your life and relationship with God? Start by being authentically you before God. You do this by exposing, in prayer, what it is more comfortable to hide. Whenever you worship God regardless of your feelings, the "real you" emerges. Picking up your Bible and reading until peace settles over you, even if it takes an hour or more, is a response to who you truly are. Be "you" and watch his grace captivate your heart. His goodness will summon you to a better way.

The Man after God's Own Heart

I know of a tremendous spiritual leader who unfortunately compromised and adapted to the very things that would attempt to knock him out of the spiritual chase. Somewhere along the way he developed a "new normal" as well. He took advantage of a woman, destroyed lives, broke God's heart, then went even further and committed murder. He listened to the wrong voice. This voice speaks in a way that makes us justify compromise and call it grace, or excuse our spiritual decline and call it balance. For us to realize just how powerful it was for Legion to ignore thousands of voices and run to Jesus on the shore of Gadara, let's consider how one mere voice brought down the mightiest of kings.

There are instances in the Bible when you simply have to slow down and reflect on the gravity of the moment. Second Samuel 11:27 is one of those verses. It says, "But the thing that David had done displeased the LORD." Well, who was David, and what did he do?

We are introduced to David in 1 Samuel 16 when, as a young shepherd boy, he was handpicked by God to become the king over ancient Israel and was anointed by the prophet Samuel. If anyone knew what it was like to be overlooked, ignored, and forgotten, it was David. He was the smallest and least likely of Jesse's sons. But God found the young man when nobody else was looking for him. God has a habit of finding you and me too.

Though chosen to be king, David did not move into the king's palace. He returned to the shepherding life and a situation that did not line up with God's promise. As I wrote in *Grace in the Valley*, we can see, through Psalm 23, that David learned to trust God even when his situation gave him reason not to.

One day after his anointing, while delivering groceries to a battle line, where the entire Israelite army was camped and facing war, death, and potential enslavement by the Philistine army, David heard the taunts of a giant named Goliath. No one supported David when he, fed up with the giant's insults toward Yahweh, spoke up and volunteered to fight. Even King Saul tried to dissuade David. Seeing David was determined to do the right but inconvenient thing, Saul then offered David his own armor for protection. David refused. Oh, how often, when we have an opportunity to perform and appear to be someone much greater and influential than we really are, do we wear the king's armor? But David was content with being himself.

Perhaps this is why God used him to bring down the giant. After all, God does not anoint who we pretend to be or who others perceive us to be. God anoints who we were created to be.

David was the one known to be the fulfillment of 1 Samuel 13:14, as God "sought out a man after his own heart." David's authenticity and heart for God come out in the psalms. He learned how to depend on God daily for mere survival during those years when King Saul pursued him around Horesh. After Saul's death, when David at last assumed the throne, Judah and Israel united and began to war with the surrounding kingdoms. God kept every promise made to David. There wasn't an area in the entire kingdom of Israel that wasn't experiencing the favor of God's blessing. The spiritual life of Israel was strong, the economy was booming, the military was well-trained and victorious, and peace finally existed in the king's palace. And God gave David "rest from all his surrounding enemies" (2 Sam. 7:1).

David had repeatedly done the honorable thing when those around him did not, and he was finally able to enjoy the rhythm of life and the comforts of royalty, for as king he had access to all his heart desired. David became used to God's goodness—but something went wrong, deep within his soul, and he didn't realize it. David was not self-aware.

Perhaps as the national ruler he lost his gratitude and became a little entitled. The fear of losing his kingdom may have created an unnecessary desire for power and control. His married life was not healthy. I wonder if he realized this. A heaviness seemed to settle down over his emotions as his soul was no longer guarded against lust and his posture was no longer wholeheartedly toward God.

In 2 Samuel 11, it was springtime in Israel. The smell of almond blossoms filled the mornings and the sunsets were painted with pastels. Years before, David had shown disdain for God's design in marriage, for as a king he had multiple wives and concubines (1 Sam. 25:42–43; 2 Sam. 3:2–5). That should have been a clue as to why David did not look away on that day that would change all days. Late one afternoon David "arose from his couch and was walking on the roof of the king's house" (2 Sam. 11:2), and he saw from a distance a woman bathing. The Hebrew word translated "walking" means "pacing back and forth."[4] David's soul was unsettled. We aren't exactly sure why. David may not have been either.

The Spear in the Ground

What did David do when he saw the woman bathing? Before going forward, we must look backward, for David knew how to steward his soul. He'd demonstrated a significant amount of self-control in his life. Years previous to that day, David, the one chosen by God to be king, had to flee to save his life from the insecure King Saul. At one time during this significant trial, David was hiding in a cave and Saul came in to relieve himself. In a moment, David could have taken Saul's life into his hands and all of his troubles would end. David's own friends even encouraged him and used religious language to do so. First Samuel 24:4–5 says,

> And the men of David said to him, "Here is the day of which the LORD said to you, 'Behold, I will give your enemy into your hand, and you shall do to him as it shall seem good to you.'" Then David arose and stealthily cut off a corner of Saul's robe. And afterward David's heart struck him, because he had cut off a corner of Saul's robe.

David had enough self-control to hold back and avoid striking down his enemy. And it doesn't end there. Though he dishonored Saul by clipping the king's robe, David would have another opportunity that is simply mind-blowing.

In another setting, David and Abishai were walking at night. They came across King Saul and his soldiers sleeping. A spear was stuck in the ground directly beside King Saul's head, and again religious language was used by a friend of David to justify something contrary to God's heart.

> Then Abishai said to David, "God has given your enemy into your hand this day. Now please let me pin him to the earth with one stroke of the spear, and I will not strike him twice." But David said to Abishai, "Do not destroy him, for who can put out his hand against the LORD's anointed and be guiltless?" And David said, "As the LORD lives, the LORD will strike him, or his day will come to die, or he will go down into battle and perish. The LORD forbid that I should put out my hand against the LORD's anointed. But take now the spear that is at his head and the jar of water and let us go." So David took the spear and the jar of water from Saul's head, and they went away. No man saw it or knew it, nor did any awake, for they were all asleep, because a deep sleep from the LORD had fallen upon them. (26:8–12)

Did you catch that last verse? It says, "a deep sleep from the LORD had fallen upon them." The Lord basically incapacitated King Saul and his soldiers, and conveniently set a weapon right by the head of David's pursuer. God even gave David a trusted friend to give not wise counsel but a mere opinion. In this we see some tests do come from the Lord, not to tempt us but to reveal what is deep within our soul. What did David do?

He did the right thing and, learning from the dishonor he'd demonstrated while cutting Saul's robe previously, exhibited a significant amount of self-control.

In 1 Samuel 27, David battled depression and aligned himself with an enemy of Israel for a time. His emotions were up and down, but he always came back to the center. David won some military conflicts as a leader and suffered disappointment when the families of his soldiers were placed in death's path. When King Saul died, David's response was to mourn and pray. The insecure leader who created so much pain for David was still honored by the former shepherd boy. At about the age of thirty, David came out of the desert after passing multiple tests. Rather than rushing to the throne to become king, David sought the Lord for his timing and wisdom. He was entrusted with part of God's promise as he began to rule as king over one-twelfth of what Saul had ruled. Eventually the entire kingdom would come to David in 2 Samuel 5:1–3.

At the apex of unprecedented blessing in his nation in 2 Samuel 11, David sees this bathing woman, whose name is Bathsheba, sends for her, and commits adultery with her. As if this wasn't horrific enough, after finding out Bathsheba was pregnant, David then issues the order for her husband, who was fighting in David's army, to be murdered.

This is what 2 Samuel 11:27 is referring to. This is what David did that was so displeasing to the Lord. If it wasn't a lack of self-control that motivated King David to commit such a heinous crime, then what was it?

Self-blindness. Søren Kierkegaard said, "Of all deceivers fear most yourself!"[5] The thoughts and dispositions within us create and work whether we realize it or not. Self-awareness, when ignored over time, sabotages our opportunity to experience real and positive change within our soul. It is almost as if we place our identity in solitary confinement and perform for the world around us. Jesus alluded to this when he described highly religious people whose lack of self-awareness influenced those around them. They were "the blind leading the blind" (see Matt. 15:14).

————

Being aware seems to be a rarity these days. You may remember the following story from the online article or evening news. If you forgot, it is likely because school shootings are commonplace, unfortunately, in our age. After all, the United States has had "fifty-seven times as many school shootings as the other major industrialized nations *combined*."[6]

Nikolas Cruz, a nineteen-year-old former student at Marjory Stoneman Douglas High School in Parkland, Florida, was the killer behind the massacre that took seventeen lives at the school. Months before the rampage, law enforcement received a tip about a social media comment where the shooter stated his aspiration to be a "professional school shooter." Somehow, he was undetected and undiscoverable, and preventative measures were not taken because people were unaware of who Nikolas was.[7]

This is very different from what happened with Joshua Alexander O'Connor. In another state, and another story, this student in Washington state was arrested and a school shooting averted after authorities received a report on a credible threat from his grandmother. This grandmother, after reading her grandson's journal and discovering a rifle in the young man's guitar case, prevented a tragedy from occurring. It appears Joshua flipped a coin to determine which school he would target. But this school never experienced what those at Marjory Stoneman Douglas High School did—because someone was aware.[8]

When the Prophet Knocks

King David moved on after the murder of Bathsheba's husband. Whether he felt remorse is yet to be discovered. Somehow, someway, David resumed his duties as king. A child of illegitimate birth would grow within the womb of the grieving Bathsheba as David enjoyed meals with her in his palace and spent time with his friends. The kingdom continued to thrive. Life eventually returned to normal. That's when the knock at the door, recorded in 2 Samuel 12:1–7, came.

When the prophet knocks at your door, do you have something to hide? David did, but it appears his heart was so calloused he'd forgotten about his crime. Perhaps God had tried knocking on his door long before and, day after day, David had ignored the sound until his heart grew hardened. I'm sure the first time God knocked, long before David committed the crime, David heard it loud and clear. He obviously ignored God. As David sent for Bathsheba after watching her from the rooftop, yet again God knocked and David ignored him. David heard the knock again when he and Bathsheba saw one another in person. God continued knocking when Bathsheba left David's presence. The knock thundered when David gave the order to murder her husband, Uriah. Time and again, God had knocked, but David never answered.

There can come a time when God knocks. But just because you don't hear it doesn't mean God forgets about it. God still calls out to us, and our hardened hearts no longer hear it. This is why Scripture says, "Today, if you hear God's voice, do not harden your hearts" (Heb. 3:15). If you do harden your heart, tomorrow God may still call, but you may not hear. God thunders, God speaks, God whispers—and though God's volume never changes, we believe it does. God's voice isn't faint; our hearts simply grow hard. There is an old Jewish saying that goes like this: "The same sun that melts the wax hardens the clay."

Samuel knocked one year after the crime. That is a long time for David to get used to what lurked in the darkness, isn't it? The prophet sought to raise his awareness of something important. He began by doing two things: telling David a story and inserting David into the story. The truth is always revealed, eventually, in the story of how things unfold. Those who seek to cover up their misdeeds by hiding them will surely be disappointed (Num. 32:23). Those who have been mistreated will one day be vindicated.

Samuel's story began with two men in a "certain city," a rich man and a poor man. In the real-life events recorded in 2 Samuel 11, there are three primary characters: David, Uriah, and Bathsheba. Samuel's story begins to make sense, doesn't it? You have the rich man, who is obviously David. The Hebrew word for "rich man" is *ashiyr*. It comes from a word meaning "rich" (literally and figuratively) and also means "noble."[9] The rich man could afford a thousand ewe lambs for he had not one flock but many. The "poor man," or *ruwsh*, is a word that comes from a primitive root meaning "to be destitute."[10]

When Samuel describes the poor man as having nothing, it is much more than how you or I understand what "nothing" means. We say things like there is *nothing* to eat when our refrigerator is full of food. Or there is *nothing* on TV though we have 562 channels and countless movie apps on our smart televisions. Our children say, "Mom, Dad, I am bored because there is *nothing* to do." That's when the proverbial "You have a garage full of sports equipment, a room full of toys, a shelf full of books, a closet full of board games and puzzles, a new video game I just purchased for your birthday, a bike and skateboard in the hallway, and a yard with neighbors to play with" speech commences.

No—the poor man's *nothing* is much different from what you and I can fathom. I have been to places where there was *nothing*. I serve with an amazing group of people at Convoy of Hope (www.convoyofhope.org). We wake up in the morning, each and every day, and believe it is possible to change the world. On a recent trip to India, I met people who literally had *no things*. Their feet did not have shoes. Their stomachs did not have food in them. Their eyes were empty from living in the city dump for decades. Their smiles left long ago. They had no hope.

The poor man literally had *no thing* except one small ewe lamb according to Samuel's story. This man was destitute, hungry, hopeless—and the little he had was stolen from him. Stolen not by a bandit beside the road or by a thief in the dark but by a rich man who could simply walk among one of his many flocks and select any lamb of his choosing. The lamb, or *kibsah*,[11] is the feminine form of the word for lamb, intentionally chosen by the prophet. Did David see that which was hidden in darkness begin to emerge in the story? Unfortunately, we find no evidence this occurred.

The poor man raised the lamb with his children. It was more than an animal; it was part of his family. The poor man fed a portion of what little food he had to the lamb. He held the lamb and it "was like a daughter to him" (2 Sam. 12:3). The

Hebrew word for "daughter" is *bath*.[12] David should have felt the sting of this in his heart. *Bath* and *Bathsheba* are too similar for anyone to miss. Yet David still did not understand. His soul was blind.

Samuel matches the characters in the story with David, Uriah, and Bathsheba. Then Samuel adds a fourth character to his parable: the traveler.

The Traveler

Memories, patterns, habits, thoughts, beliefs, and emotional and mental baggage are brought by travelers. Often, we do not know when they begin walking the path with us and, too often, we do not see them by our side. We take our children to the park and the traveler comes. We go out with our friends to the movies and dinner, and the four of us have a fifth, though unseen, joining. People walk down the aisle to get married and, as they leave to begin the honeymoon, they are surprised when marital problems begin. They wonder if getting married was a mistake, failing to realize the traveler brings problems, often undetected, to the marriage.

We go from job to job, city to city, and never fully learn how to function in life because we think everyone else is the problem. We leave our church, attend another one, and leave shortly thereafter, because the traveler is hungry. We sneak away to abuse substances on the traveler's behalf. Anxiety and depression grip us for yet another day because the traveler must eat. We pray and feel like we are talking to a wall. We read the Bible and can't seem to get anywhere in our faith. We feel alone in crowded rooms. We volunteer at church or in our community and it just isn't enough. We say things we should never say. We commit sins and call it freedom. We suffer from spiritual decay and call it relevance. We change our opinion based on who is in the room. We do not confront in healthy ways because we would rather be accepted by everyone than have authentic, real relationships with a few. We believe lies about ourselves. We do the very things our parents did that we swore we never would. Shame may torment us, religious performance can deceive us, our past often defines us, and our future intimidates us. Why? The traveler must eat, and its insatiable appetite is never fully and completely satisfied.

The traveler is no respecter of persons, for we all have one. The traveler studies us and knows us well.

The traveler blended into David's life well because David had a religious veneer. Second Samuel 6 records the story of David bringing the ark of the covenant back to Jerusalem. The ark was a religious symbol that represented the presence of God and served as a constant reminder of God's holiness. When the ark was in the possession of the Israelites, they were successful in military campaigns. Surrounding nations heard the stories and some visibly saw supernatural displays when the ark was around. For David, bringing the ark back to Jerusalem in less than a day's journey was significant to his kingdom's future and a return to what mattered most.

David was a passionate lover of God. In this story, he set aside his title and accolades by disrobing from his royal attire. He danced and worshiped radically before God and Israel's people as the ark was carried back to the royal city. Scripture says David alone danced. David didn't become a slave to the crowd's opinion. His love for God shaped where he placed his priorities. Every six steps, David sacrificed animals (v. 13), the modern-day equivalent of spending thousands of dollars.

By the time the ark arrived, millions of dollars had been invested as an offering to God. David was known and seen as a God-loving king. He was not pretending nor was he being fake. David danced before God with all of his might because of who God was to him. David's own wife criticized him and despised him (v. 16) for his worship of God, yet he did not compromise.

David demonstrated in this story a significant amount of self-control and commitment to his Lord. Yet I suggest that even during this time David danced, the traveler was near.

As Samuel continued telling David his parable, he said, "Now there came a traveler to the rich man, and he was unwilling to take one of his own flock or herd to prepare for the guest who had come to him, but he took the poor man's lamb and prepared it for the man who had come to him" (12:4).

This traveler, or *helek*, came not to the poor man but to the rich one. The word means "journey, wayfarer, and flowing."[13] *Flowing* is a word picture describing a reservoir with the dam opening up. Unwilling to take one lamb from his own flock, the rich man stole the ewe lamb from the poor man. Why did the rich man steal the lamb from the poor man? To feed the traveler. But who is this traveler? In the Talmud and the writings of Augustine, for example, there is a distinction between the three different descriptions of the allegorical character in verse 4, each representing something tugging at David's soul.

First, "a traveler" walks past and around the rich man and lodges elsewhere. Then, after time, "the guest" stays with the rich man temporarily. Eventually, "the man who had come to him" will become a permanent resident in the rich man's home. The presence of the traveler is something we must all be aware of in order to deal with it and prevent it from becoming a permanent resident with us.[14]

———————

One voice, spoken by the traveler, brought down the mightiest of kings. Thousands of voices, echoing within the soul of the one they called Legion in Mark 5, could not hold the man back from pursuing Jesus with all of his soul. What was the difference between David and the man in Mark 5? They both fixed their gaze on a destination and both ran with all of their might in that direction. David ran after something that looked good, felt good, and satisfied the traveler. But Legion ran after Jesus.

If our sacred chase today, tomorrow, or ten years from now ends up anywhere other than face-to-face with God, we run in vain. You may read this and have every reason to think God gave up on you, isn't interested in you, or that your life is too much of a mess for anything beautiful to come from it. God loves you and picks you up when you fall down in your race. Or maybe you have been seduced by opportunities that have slowly weaned you away from pursuing God wholeheartedly and you now realize you're ready to grow closer to God than ever before.

Regardless of where you are, start now, for Jesus has come ashore.

The man called Legion had thousands of travelers accompany him on that rocky path toward the seashore of Gadara, but he surrendered to the deep longing in his soul for a greater connection with God, and he began his chase after Jesus rode the winds on the sea to chase after him. It is possible to position your heart in such a way that God's best becomes your new normal. And if your family members, friends, or even strangers go looking in your spiritual attic one day and dust off an old, tattered scrapbook of your life, like Mr. Winton, you will be able to say that a heaven-soaked life on earth really doesn't seem that abnormal after all.

CHAPTER SIX

God Speaks a Better Word

A few years ago, I had an experience that our two girls
thought was pretty amazing. I was invited to California
with a small group of about twenty leaders for a strategic gathering. After a day of conversation and planning, we postponed
our agenda for dinner at a nice seafood restaurant. I invest a
lot of time in meetings and speaking, so at a dinner like that,
while everyone else is gabbing away and doing their network-
ing, I typically resort to one of two things: (1) I either pick
one person and share a conversation with them about Jesus
and life; or, (2) I put my head down, eat my salmon, and save
the remaining words I have left in my heart for my phone call
home to Ali. Well, this time I sat next to a guy who was a movie
star and had recently become a Christ follower. He had a lot
of questions, and we spent two hours talking about why and
how the pursuit of Jesus is worth it. For dessert, we all skipped
the cake and exchanged it for a private tour of Marvel Studios
thanks to a friend.

Being able to tour a facility where TV shows and movies are made would create a good story to share with Ali and the girls when I got home. In the studios, I found the set designs and technology impressive, though I was not familiar with half of the shows and movies they said were created in each one. We were forbidden to take photos or video footage for obvious reasons, and though I understood, I was disappointed because I was eager to show our girls what things looked like.

But after we were all rescued by the fire department in an unexpected turn of events at Marvel, I had something even better to share with my family upon returning home. Let's just say you can tell a lot about a person when you are stuck in an elevator with them, in California, in the heat, for a long, long time.

We had filed into the square metal box and were about to dangle in the air with the sheer support of a few metal cables as our tour took us to yet another "must-see" room. I guarantee no one thought we would get stuck in the elevator until, after the door closed, someone said, "What is the occupancy limit on this thing, anyway?" We were crammed like sardines. I was one of the first individuals to get on and they just kept coming and coming and coming.

Sure enough, after a few seconds of elevator travel, we heard a loud thud and were all jolted to an abrupt halt. A few of the passengers looked around in bewilderment, others sighed, some moaned, and two screamed. I'm sure one of my eyebrows crawled to the top of my forehead. This was my first—and hopefully last—experience of being stuck in an elevator.

Most of the passengers were part of the meeting I'd been in earlier that day. There were PhDs, corporate leaders, entertainment industry millionaires, a few pastors, and others I can't really remember. The jokes and laughs didn't last long because one of the gentlemen, who was wearing a rather nice suit, began sweating profusely and took off his coat. He'd used words in our meeting I had to look up online to find out what he was saying, but all dignity and sophistication went out of the window—or should I say, out the small crack between the two steel panels of the elevator door.

This scientist ripped off his necktie next, untucked his shirt, and began panicking. I watched as others began to do the same while the temperature and humidity crept up and the oxygen level slowly decreased. In a few minutes, the scientist was on his knees with his mouth up to the crack in the doors trying to suck in additional oxygen. He was terrified. Someone tried to hit the red emergency button. I am not sure if it ever worked. Your mind goes to some unique places when you're stuck on an elevator. I prayed silently and remained calm as I sweat through my clothes. We were all drenched by the time the fire department pried open the doors. Everyone verbally expressed their appreciation, some cheered, others applauded—and the scientist rolled out of the elevator in what I can only assume was sheer delight.

After I had asked a firefighter for a photo to share with my family, one of the first responders asked me, "Sir, what is your name?" It appears they needed some information for a report or to keep track of who was rescued. I thought nothing of it. "My name is Heath Adamson," I replied. There, that wasn't so bad now, was it?

"What's your name?" is typically not a mind-boggling question for any of us. But for the man they called Legion, who overcame all excuses and started his sacred chase toward Jesus, this same question revealed an awful lot, for the man had no idea who he truly was.

We Are Many

Our identity is not who people perceive us to be. It is who God knows us to be (2 Cor. 5:11). When we lack ongoing connection with God after our salvation moment, we can project an image of who we want others to think we are. But if we don't chase God to keep catching another glimpse of who we truly are in his eyes, we will end up performing and living an artificial life to gain an inferior promise from the world.

Additionally, our identity is not who we pretend to be. We must refuse to be enslaved by the need for approval from others. This is why Paul wrote in Galatians 1:10, "For am I now seeking the approval of man, or of God? Or am I trying to please man?"

Who we are is equivalent to who we belong to. As followers of Christ, you and I belong to an amazing Father called God. Jesus modeled this well for us. When Jesus performed his first public miracle at a wedding in Cana of Galilee, it was Mary, his mother, who brought the need for more wine to Jesus's attention (John 2). Jesus replied that it wasn't his time yet, and then Mary looked at a group of people and basically said, "Just do whatever Jesus tells you to do." Before you know it, Jesus turned water into wine. Why did Mary come to Jesus expecting him to do something miraculous and instantaneous? I believe it was because Jesus performed many miracles at home and around his family that the public never saw—but Mary did. Even then, though Mary believed, the Lord's other earthly family members did not. John 7:3–5 reveals that Jesus's own family didn't believe he was the Son of God, but this did not affect his identity.

You can tell a lot about a person based on the first thing they say to you when you meet. When a grandparent walks into the hospital and lays eyes on their first grandchild, you hear things like "She is so precious," or "He looks just like you, son." A grandmother doesn't walk in, pick up her brand-new grand-baby, and say, "Isn't she potty-trained yet?" After you are away for two weeks on a trip and are greeted at the airport by your family, they don't respond with "Why did you come back?"

No, they usually say something like "We missed you so much." The first words out of someone's mouth reflect what is important to them in the moment and what they have been thinking about related to the situation. When the man they called Legion ran toward the Lord, he was asked a simple question by the Son of God: "What's your name?"

Mark 5:6–9 picks up the story:

> And when he saw Jesus from afar, he ran and fell down before him. And crying out with a loud voice, he said, "What have you to do with me, Jesus, Son of the Most High God? I adjure you by God, do not torment me." For he was saying to him, "Come out of the man, you unclean spirit!" And Jesus asked him, "What is your name?" He replied, "My name is Legion, for we are many."

Jesus was not interested in carrying on a conversation about the issues this man was plagued with. Jesus wanted to speak directly to the person created in God's image.

Jesus didn't ask, "Where are your clothes, creep?" The Lord's response wasn't "How in the world did you get so messed up?" Jesus looked at the one who they tried to bind with chains and tame, and whose screams lulled the Gadarene children to sleep at night, and wanted to know his name. Names in Scripture were significant. They had meaning, were relevant to the individual's destiny, and often were prophetic. When someone acknowledged their name in Scripture, it was tied to all of these realities.

For example, in Genesis 27, Jacob pretended to be his brother Esau and sought to inherit his brother's blessing from his father, Isaac. When asked who he truly was, Jacob deceived Isaac. For years, Jacob lived a life that appeared to be successful, but it was based on a lie. In Genesis 32, he wrestled with God. In the story, God also asked for his name and, contrary to pretending to be Esau as he had earlier, Jacob acknowledged who he really was. Jacob's vulnerability unlocked his true identity in God, and his name was changed to *Israel*, which means "God contends" and "persevere."[1]

The source of our struggle is often a clue to the next step in our sacred chase. The first step to a greater connection with God is setting aside the excuses, shame, and distractions to pursue him. This means being authentic, truly revealing how we think and feel to God. It means being unashamed and daring to believe God will not turn us away, just like Jesus didn't turn Legion away. This is authenticity at its best. Then the next step is to continue by being intentionally vulnerable with God in the deepest part of your soul. In doing this, you choose to dare to believe God's significant, custom-designed purpose is worth all of your attention.

There is a freedom that changes everything when we take off our mask and let God into those areas he was aware of all along. Legion's response to Jesus wasn't, "Oh, you know, my name is Bob, and I was just in the neighborhood and wanted to stop and say hello." Can you imagine how vulnerable you need to be to look at God and admit you don't really remember who you are anymore? What I deeply appreciate about the man they called Legion is that he was able to articulate who he thought he was rather than performing. When Jesus asked the man what his name was, he was trying to reorient the man to look toward what God thinks and says about him and finally let go of the lies he had believed.

What lies have you believed about yourself?

You may think God forgives everyone else, but that you—well, you are a different story. You may believe your struggle has just been too long and too hard for even God to bring you through. You may tolerate less than what God promised because you don't think you deserve it. You may believe God answers everyone else's prayers but yours. You may feel guilty because in the past you tried to pursue God with all of your soul and fell flat on your face. Now, trying again is much more difficult than quitting, so you sacrifice your deep desire to connect on a deeper level with God to the idol of convenience.

There is a reality you must embrace that will take you into your full spiritual inheritance. What is it? *God's love for you is greater than everything else that comes against you.* Romans 8:31 says, "If God is for us, who can be against us?" You are a child of Almighty God. Don't let shame persuade you to bow out of the race to pursue God even more. Shame was the culprit in the garden of Eden, and it still tries to hold us back today.

Where Are You? Who Told You?

One of the most recognizable stories in the Bible is found in Genesis 3, when Adam and Eve eat the forbidden fruit from the tree of the knowledge of good and evil. Adam was instructed in Genesis 2 to cultivate the earth and meet his needs in tandem with God's process. This is interesting, since God could easily have fed Adam supernaturally. God did so with the Israelites in the exodus, and he also used ravens to feed Elijah. Sometimes, though God can do something instantaneously, he chooses to act progressively. Both are miraculous.

Holding the fruit in their hands was yet another reminder to trust God's process, but Adam and Eve wanted to gain instantaneous access to their desire. They disregarded God's best and ate the forbidden fruit.

This subtle and seemingly insignificant act of disobedience opened up a torrent of brokenness that flooded the earth. When sin entered our world, so did all of its friends. Humankind was created to never become sick and die. However, disease, deformity, and death began when Adam and Eve ate the forbidden fruit. Created to live in a family where Mom and Dad kept their word, now children are exposed to divorce and all types of abuse. Originally formed by God to live in safety and dignity, innocent children are captive to child prostitution, men and women are captive to pornography, and young and old alike are captive to the guilt that comes with abortion, all because of sin.

People are diagnosed with leukemia because Adam and Eve ate from the tree. Depression haunts people because of the disobedience in the garden of Eden. Every word spoken that creates confusion and pain originated in that decision. The worst consequence of Adam and Eve's disobedience was not physical, however. It was spiritual. Sin separates us from God. Their choice created a chasm between God and humanity that no one could cross. I am thankful for the gospel and that, in our sinful state, Jesus still thought us worthy enough to die for.

Immediately after eating the fruit, Adam and Eve knew they had disobeyed, for Genesis 3:7 says, "The eyes of both were opened, and they knew that they were naked. And they sewed fig leaves together and made themselves loincloths." Their first realization was that they were naked. What is interesting is that they did not become naked after they sinned; rather, they became ashamed of their nakedness after they sinned.

Shame was the first observable consequence in the garden.

Their response was to try to cover themselves and hide. Think about that for a moment. They were ashamed and hid from God. I would suggest that whenever we close off a part of our soul to God by not pursuing him with all of our heart, we do it because of shame. Shame says, *You aren't good enough and you certainly aren't worth it.* It tries to convince us not only that something is wrong with us but that we are the problem. Shame is all about *self.* Scripture does not tell us to "fix our eyes on ourselves." We are supposed to fix our eyes on Jesus. If Legion fixed his eyes on himself, he would have never taken that next step to draw near and replace proximity with intimacy. When we gaze upon Jesus, like Legion did while crying out in the limestone caves of Gadara, we will never experience disappointment or embarrassment in God's eyes.

If I were God, when I knew Adam and Eve had eaten the fruit, and sin and death had entered the world, I would think long and hard about what I would say to them when we first came in contact after the sin. Did God scold them? Did God accuse them? No.

Now, I want to be clear: God did allow judgment to enter the world as a consequence of their sin. God certainly did not excuse it. Sin cannot be ignored or merely apologized for. It must be atoned for, and our only hope is in Jesus Christ. But God's initial response, as the first humans cowered and hid from him, was to address their shame and its relationship to drawing identity from the wrong voice.

They heard the sound of the LORD God walking in the garden in the cool of the day, and the man and his wife hid themselves from the presence of the LORD God among the trees of the garden. But the LORD God called to the man and said to him, "Where are you?" And he said, "I heard the sound of you in the garden, and I was afraid, because I was naked, and I hid myself." He said, "Who told you that you were naked? Have you eaten of the tree of which I commanded you not to eat?" (vv. 8–11)

Adam and Eve heard the sound not only of God's voice but of God walking. They distinctly knew the sound of God's feet hitting the ground in an environment teeming with a variety of other animals, both big and small. It is possible to know God in such an intimate way that we hear his walk long before we see him. When we spend time in conversation with God, what we talked about yesterday informs today. When we read Scripture, those words come into our mind at just the right time and provide direction and hope. In these ways and more, we learn to identify God's steps and can hear him drawing near once again.

When it says God came walking in the "cool of the day," the Hebrew word for "cool" is *ruach*.[2] This word is also translated in the Old Testament as "spirit." This refers not only to the time of day, which according to Hebrew commentaries was during the windy evening, but also to the form God took in coming to Adam and Eve. God came to them not in the form of the Father or Son but the form of the Holy Spirit. This is important. The Holy Spirit is still God's initial response to us when our true identity is compromised.

As they hid from God, with plenty of time to think of what his response to them would be now that wickedness and evil had entered the world, God called out and asked where they were. God obviously knew the answer. He is God. But the question is much more than rhetorical. It reveals something deep and profound. God created them to be perfect—in the divine image and for connection to God. But this was now absent. Their God-given identity was corrupted, and though God knew where they were physically, it's almost as if their new identity disguised by shame made them unrecognizable to him. Adam responded with honesty to God's question, and God's second question is even more revealing. "Who told you that you were naked?" (v. 11). God's first concern was not that the door to cancer, sexual abuse, murder, anxiety, corporate greed, war, racism, and all other sins had been opened. God's first concern was their unrecognizable identity because of shame and his second concern was that Adam (and Eve) listened to a voice other than God's tell them something about themselves.

Now we understand why Jesus asked the demonized man who lived in Gadara who he was. There is an inseparable link between deeply connecting with God and eliminating the confusion of who God created us to be. One of the most important truths that serves as a compass for us on our God-journey, ensuring we always head in the right direction, is refusing to keep secrets with the devil. This means we have to be transparent with God.

We are meant to be good stewards of our soul, just like we expect our bank or credit union to be a good steward of our paycheck when it is deposited. We pay close attention to the deposits we make into our heart, for one day we all must make a withdrawal. When we take out more than we deposit, hopelessness is born, and this hopelessness will sabotage us in our pursuit. Legion, in his hopelessness, still partnered with his desire to know God. Legion did not allow his issues to influence his pursuit. Draper Kauffman didn't either.

SEALs

A few years ago I was in Southern California for some meetings. The hotel was a few miles away from a US Naval base where Navy SEALs train and qualify for the elite group. One morning I saw some of the soldiers running along the beach holding what appeared to be something bulky over their heads. As I got closer, I could see they were carrying large, heavy backpacks. I saw a few other soldiers yelling at them as they ran. There is something pretty cool about watching soldiers train like that. I am thankful for those who serve and protect our land. The SEALs, arguably one of the most elite fighting groups in the world we know of, developed not from a grand strategy of the military but, according to what I can find, from one individual who refused to allow his condition to keep him from moving ahead. His name was Draper Kauffman, and today he is known as the godfather of the US Navy SEALs.[3]

With a military career full of life-threatening scenarios, heroic and uncelebrated missions, and war, Kauffman's most unbelievable achievement is something that the history books can't quite measure. It is also something each one of us possesses within our own soul if we will learn to listen to not the loudest voice in our heart but the most important one.

In 1933, upon his graduation from the Naval academy, Kauffman's expected road to go down would be receiving an officer's commission. His plan was to follow in the footsteps of another great man, his father, who also served in the US Navy. But it wasn't to be.

It was not because of drug abuse that Kauffman's dreams were shattered, nor was it because of a life of crime. He simply had poor eyesight and this, according to the Navy, was enough to prevent him from receiving his commission. What do you do when you invest years of emotional energy dreaming about a bright future and making plans to get there, only to find it sabotaged by something surprising, something shocking—and something that to you seems so small? This is where Kauffman can inspire us all. The final draft of the story is never final. Even after it is written.

With his door to the US Navy closed, he moved to Berlin in 1939 and then joined the American Volunteer Ambulance Corps in France. This warrior trained to lead other warriors into combat found himself behind the wheel of an ambulance. He was imprisoned for a short time in France when the Germans occupied the country in 1940. After his release, he joined the Royal Navy Reserve in England and served in their bomb disposal unit. While he was home on leave, the US Navy sought him out to learn from his experiences. At their request Kauffman organized and ran an underwater demolition school with the purpose of not destroying but saving lives.

The school Kauffman was in charge of took form off the coast of Florida. After the United States entered the war because of the events at Pearl Harbor, Kauffman's experience and trainees became crucial to US amphibious operations around the world. To keep the reality of their work from being known by the enemy, these "frogmen" were not honored publicly for their efforts, such as disarming underwater bombs or conducting top-secret reconnaissance, in changing the course of the war. Though most of the world is now aware of the SEALS, during WWII most of their work with Kauffman was kept secret. Had Kauffman allowed poor eyesight to be the final draft of his identity, serving as the label for his purpose and the issue that defined his potential, the Allies' strategy during WWII would have been different.

Accused No More

An accusation is when we are "charged with wrongdoing."⁴ The battleground of spiritual accusation is unseen, though the casualties are observable in airports, churches, work environments, and even at kitchen tables. I can't find evidence that Kauffman was accused of poor eyesight, however, when crisis hit and the need to find solutions to win the war became more important than the need to find reasons to disqualify. I do know, because it is the universal human condition, that he would have had to deal with that seductive voice in his head telling him he wasn't qualified to be a hero because he couldn't pass the eye exam. Our heart, when filled with insecurity, defeat, excuses, and pain, accuses us frequently. When filled with the hope found in God's promises, however, our heart propels us forward, no longer dwelling on the problems around us but instead focusing on the amazing journey in front of us.

It isn't enough, though, for our heart to lead us in the right direction. We must choose to move.

Psalm 27:8 says, "You have said, 'Seek my face.' My heart says to you, 'Your face, LORD, do I seek.'" David, who wrote this psalm, heard God say to seek his face. Exodus 33:20 records God telling Moses that "you cannot see my face, for man shall not see me and live." David would have known this verse. For God to say what he did to David is astounding. What in a previous generation was impossible, through David's vulnerability and honesty before God, became possible. We have an invitation by God to seek the divine face and go on the sacred chase, but we must declare boldly that we not only accept this invitation but will do something about it. The enemy of our soul knows the power of hope, which is why our identity in Christ is a constant target. When Jesus asked the man what his name was in Mark 5, he showed that God is much more focused on our identity than our issues. After all, our issues flow from our understanding and application of who we are in him.

When Satan tried to destroy the purpose for which Jesus of Nazareth came to earth, he did not hire an assassin or try to inundate his body with an incurable virus. His strategy was to come discreetly to Jesus after the Lord's baptism, where Jesus heard the Father say he was God's beloved Son (Matt. 3:17). Satan, knowing who Jesus was since before God created humanity, met Jesus in the barren wilderness and offered him an interesting proposition: "If you are the Son of God, command this stone to become bread" (Luke 4:3). The Passion Translation puts it this way: "If you are really the Son of God, command this stone to turn into a loaf of bread for you." Jesus could have been tempted to perform to validate his identity and justify his existence. Satan attacked Jesus's identity both directly and indirectly, not just once but three times (Matt. 4:3, 6, and 9). Satan's tactic was to use identity to disqualify Jesus from continuing his race. During Jesus's life, we don't see a lot of disagreement over whether Jesus really performed miracles. We do see a lot of discussion over whether Jesus was truly who he said he was.

In the same way Satan tempted and accused Jesus, our experience really is no different. Job 1:9–2:6 reveals that Satan came before God to accuse Job of serving God with impure motives. Job's love for God and pursuit of God's heart were not aborted because of this accusation. Job pressed forward and, in the end, showed that a realm of intimacy with God is found when we continue loving and worshiping God even when our heart may tell us we have reason not to (Job 42:10). There is another story in the Old Testament where Satan again appeared before God to accuse Joshua the high priest (Zech. 3:1). But after Jesus died on the cross, Scripture does not record any instance when Satan appears in God's presence to accuse anyone else. Why?

After his resurrection from the dead, Jesus sat down at the right hand of the Father (Eph. 1:20–23). It is there where Jesus makes intercession for us (Heb. 7:25). "God's right hand," a phrase found throughout the Bible, is the place of God's highest favor (Exod. 15:6; Isa. 48:13). It's almost as if when Satan, who is our accuser (Rev. 12:9–11), tries to drive a wedge between God's goodness and our privilege of inheriting God's prom-ise, Jesus is there to point to the work he did on the cross and how, once and for all, we can live as sons or daughters of the King. If Satan can no longer come before God and accuse us, though he is still the accuser of God's people, then how does his accusation work today?

Satan gains access to us not through force but through our thoughts. Those of us who are seated with Christ in heavenly places (Eph. 2:6–7) actually end up accusing ourselves. When-ever we dwell on a thought about ourselves or our reality that God does not have, we partner with it and exchange truth for a lie (Rom. 1:25). For example, we can think that because we did not pray correctly or enough, our promise is no longer available. When Jesus asks us what our name is, like he did Legion, we respond, "I am someone who didn't pray enough," and God, like he did in Genesis 3, asks, "Who told you that?" Or we may feel like God still holds our past against us simply because we still remember our failures, and when our name is inquired of by God, we say, "My name is alcoholic / depressed / overlooked / alone / fill in the blank."

Actually, when you fill in the blank, go ahead and write "son" or "daughter," because that's the only name you have.

Jesus of Nazareth is the Word of God clothed with humanity (John 1:14). Interestingly, we don't even have a word preserved that he wrote with his own hand. But we do have Scripture, where I can find three primary moments when God writes something. Two of the themes of God's writing are the law (God inscribed the Ten Commandments on stone in Deut. 4:13) and judgment (a divine hand wrote on the wall in Dan. 5). The wall would have been a hard substance similar to the tablets.

In the New Testament, we have record of Jesus writing once, not in stone but in the dirt (John 8:6–8). This is similar to what is described in Jeremiah 17:13. The woman caught in the act of adultery was about to be judged by the law. What did Jesus do? He bent down and wrote something we have no record of, and the crowd that formed to execute the adulteress with rocks began to quickly disappear. Jesus looked at her and said, "Neither do I condemn you; go, and from now on sin no more" (v. 11).

The law of God and surety of God's judgment are written in stone. When Christ writes, he is drawing attention to what his audience would be familiar with from Jeremiah. The consequences of our sins are written "on the earth," but they are easily wiped away by the divine hand for all of God's sons and daughters. The enemy of your soul accuses you from your past with the law and judgment because, if you are in Christ, there is nothing to accuse you from now.

The worst conclusion you can draw when your past is thrown in your face is that you are not who God says you are and God is not who God says he is. After David confessed his sin and dealt with his iniquity, he wrote the words of Psalm 51. Knowing the backstory behind the following words makes them even more sobering for us. For a king who had it all and tasted of God's goodness only to squander it to feed the traveler, this psalm reveals not only David's brokenness before God but also a key to get rid of the traveler once and for all. David said, "Take not your Holy Spirit from me" (Ps. 51:11). God came to Adam and Eve in the garden in the form of the Holy Spirit, and David recognized there is something important about the Spirit's role in our sacred chase.

But who is the Holy Spirit, and what does he do?

When a thousand voices try to distract you from pursuing a greater connection with God, the Spirit of God speaks truth to you. When you're depressed, God speaks hope. When you're stuck, God says there is a way forward. If you don't remember who you are anymore, God lovingly calls you his child. God always speaks a better word as the Spirit of God speaks to your heart and mind.

Although the man in Mark 5 really didn't even recognize who he truly was, rather than pretending, he was as honest as he could be. It didn't stop there, however. Being open with God is much more than talking about our struggles. It means we align our soul with who God is and who God says we are, and we allow the better word spoken to and about us, from God, to echo in our souls.

How do we know what God is saying? Well, there are a variety of ways God speaks according to Scripture. The best place to start is by reading the Bible. It is more than a religious book. It is often what God uses to bring clarity to the issues in our soul (Heb. 4:12), is always useful for any situation in life

(2 Tim. 3:15–17), and always serves as a guide to whether our thoughts and feelings are in alignment with truth (Deut. 8:3; John 1:1, 14).

We don't know what Jesus said to the man after the evil spirits entered the swine. We do know the one who called himself Legion, after speaking honestly with Jesus, experienced a transformation that is unlike anything I've ever read in the Bible. This same transformation is accessible to each one of us right now. The key for us all is hearing and responding to the Holy Spirit's whisper, just like David identified for us in Psalm 51.

CHAPTER SEVEN

When Demons Beg

I remember seeing demons beg just like it is recorded in Mark 5:12.

I was invited by a pastor I had known for years to join him in a meeting with a man I will call Pete. Pete's behavior was concerning both to himself and to others. He often stared off in space and randomly twitched as if volts of electricity surged in his body. When speaking with others, his voice would sometimes change as if multiple people lived inside him. He harmed himself. He wasn't sleeping. He had gone to physicians and other professionals, but nothing was working. During church he often jumped up from the pew and ran out in the middle of the pastor's sermon. Pete had asked the pastor if they could talk because he knew something was wrong—something beyond the physical realm.

As a young child, I was introduced to the occult and witchcraft. I saw and experienced things I will never discuss publicly. I knew beyond the shadow of a doubt that what we don't see is much more real than anything we do. After meeting Jesus and becoming free from the addictions and the darkness, I had first-hand knowledge not just of how "things on that side" worked but also how free someone could truly become in Christ. Because of my background and unique experiences with the supernatural, the pastor thought I could assist him with Pete.

We scheduled a phone call, since I lived in another city. I wanted to meet Pete and hear his heart. It was an evening, and I remember it vividly. My goal was to let Pete know there was no judgment on my end and that my sincere goal was to see him find the relief in his soul made possible by Jesus. They met in the pastor's office, and I was on speakerphone so they could both participate in our conversation. As we talked, Pete's voice changed, and it caught both the pastor and myself off guard. In a deep, raspy, slithering voice, Pete—or more accurately something or someone inside of Pete—began to say things about me that an ordinary stranger could not possibly have known. He spoke of details in my personal life and, as the pastor recalled later, suddenly stood up as his voice changed back to his own. Pete said, "It tells me to have nothing to do with that man on the phone!" Then he ran out of the pastor's office. The pastor and I were stunned. We prayed and decided to keep the face-to-face meeting we'd scheduled with Pete before the phone call ended. Hopefully, we thought, Pete would come back. Well, he did.

A few weeks later, when the three of us sat down together in person on the church campus, I noticed how Pete never looked me in the eyes. He was a larger man who appeared to be very strong. He looked like any other person. As we talked Pete began to randomly shake. He made high-pitched, nail-biting noises and began shouting obscenities. Again, he said things and knew things about me he shouldn't have known. In the next breath, Pete talked to us as if he wanted desperately to find hope again. He seemed to go back and forth between two worlds. He was hurting and crying out.

Then, without a moment's notice, his voice changed into that same voice I'd heard over the phone. It was like Pete wanted things to change but something or someone kept pulling him back. The voices inside of him argued with one another, and one voice seemed to beg and plead. I saw Pete do things that were heartbreaking. I wept. The pastor and I prayed. The name of Jesus is powerful. With the mere mention of his name, the voices stopped and Pete calmed down.

There are times when individuals suffer from multiple personality disorder or they relive a traumatic experience from the past with immense detail. It is important we don't categorize people and assume everything is a "demon." Sometimes people just need to grieve, find a safe place to talk, and process emotions. What was different about Pete was his familiarity with details in my life. There was something otherworldly about this experience—something beyond the realm of words.

Then Pete's voice changed into that of a little boy. He literally sounded like a child with the same pitch, tone, inflections, and lisp. In front of us, he relived an experience he'd had as a child, growing up in a third-world country where he experienced unspeakable things. Suddenly, Pete leaped out of his chair and lunged straight for my throat. His hands stopped a few inches away as he stretched out to strangle me.

For the first time I was able to look into his eyes. What I saw I will never forget. In that moment, as Pete was suspended in the air with his hands outstretched, I heard the peaceful voice of the Lord say inside my heart, *Even if all of hell comes for your throat I am able to stop it.* I then saw Pete get pulled back through the air, and he sat down. All of this happened within a matter of seconds. I asked Pete if he wanted to be free, and he said no, for "It was too hard to let them go." As we walked out of the room, his voice changed between that of a little boy and that of an otherworldly being. His last spoken words to me, that he didn't want to be free, were sobering.

I am thankful for modern medicine and how science has shaped our world. Where would we be without penicillin, the X-ray machine, CAT scans, or much-needed vaccines? Science helps little children who are born without a limb experience increased mobility and excel in life. Continuing research allows us to conceive of a day when cancer no longer affects so many people. Modern medicine also helps many who struggle with and through mental illness. The world of the rational and observable empowers farmers to end the cycle of physical poverty in their families by cultivating the ground underneath their feet in severe drought zones. Technology opens doors for families to unite across vast distances and share moments together. Our world is a better place because humanity continues to grow and thrive thanks to scientific, intellectual, and technological breakthroughs. I believe in learning and growing.

In the Bible, however, we see there is a spiritual realm beyond the scientific and definable. Some things just don't fit into worldly, psychological categories. In Scripture, we see that there are some things we simply cannot fully understand. Perhaps understanding should not be the ultimate goal? This is something many Western Christians struggle with, unfortunately. This is the problem: we always need a category. However, I have friends in places like Argentina, Burkina Faso, India, and the United States who have had similar experiences as mine with Pete.

The Bible is a window into a world we should not be ignorant of regardless of how modern or postmodern we are. For example, in Matthew 16:23 Jesus acknowledged that the spiritual world can often manifest in the physical one. One-quarter of Jesus's miraculous healings in the Gospel of Mark actually involved deliverances from evil spirits. There is much more to the spiritual life than what we will ever see. If we dare to believe in life after death, believing in the activity of angels and demons shouldn't be that mind-blowing. The key is to remain grounded in what the Bible teaches and avoid sensationalism.

Briefcases and Ties

Some would try to psychologically and scientifically explain the otherworldly behaviors I witnessed with Pete. It is certainly appropriate to apply knowledge, wisdom, and understanding. To apply earthly knowledge without the wisdom and understanding of God revealed in Scripture, however, is foolish. Those who berated and betrayed Jesus during his supposed trial knew a lot of information about who the Son of God would be. But they lacked understanding, and for this reason what they thought they knew actually worked against them.

Knowledge and information were designed to emerge from and receive clarity through intimacy with God. God created knowledge, and Scripture says we are destroyed without it (Hosea 4:6). The book of Proverbs is full of examples of how God gives us learning and information to excel in life and establish his promises on the earth. The knowledge of God, however, has less to do with intellectual achievement or IQ and more to do with God's heart. Judas, the one who betrayed Jesus, had all of his questions answered by Jesus himself. He sat regularly under the teaching of Jesus. Good teaching and perfect knowledge aren't enough if your heart doesn't yield to God.

The man known as Legion ran to Jesus, and the most accurate interpretation of what occurs in these verses would be this: he fell down before Jesus as the demons paid the Lord homage. The evil spirits weren't saying Jesus was *their* Lord; rather, they were admitting Jesus is *the* Lord. The demons in Mark 5 possessed knowledge. They knew exactly who Jesus was and were not ashamed or concerned with political correctness when exclaiming it. Their knowledge alone did not change anything, just like knowledge we accumulate from a classroom or degree cannot fully explain Pete's behavior.

This is a great example of how our beliefs mean nothing if they aren't applied to our lives. The man called Legion was completely overwhelmed, confused, and tormented. Again, he had thousands of excuses that should have kept him from pursuing a deeper connection with God. Somehow, he allowed his spiritual passion to fuel his actions to produce real, sustainable renewal.

Your life will be rewarded as you remember the reality of the spiritual world. It doesn't mean you need to agonize in prayer on whether to order bacon with your cheeseburger because of spirituality. It simply means an assessment of your circumstance taken without considering God's view is inferior. I often wonder if we educate and advance ourselves into a candy-coated form of spiritual deception and, in our wise and persuasive explanations, don't realize it.

A family friend of ours was born and still lives in Burkina Faso. His experiences with the unseen world are a good reminder for us all that what we see is not all there is. His doctoral work is being done at a prestigious university in England. One of his professors asked him why, in the remote parts of Africa, stories of the collision of seen and unseen worlds frequently emerge; yet when viewed from their modern, educated society, experiences like mine, our friend's, and the one they called Legion seem too remarkable to be true. His response is something we can all learn from. He said, "In Africa, you say our devils have pitchforks and tails. In your country, they often carry briefcases and wear ties."

What is he saying? We are surrounded by the supernatural and, regardless of how well-educated or scientifically advanced we are, there is still more to life than what we can understand and at times even prove. In our modern, Western world, we have higher education, more wealth, and the most advanced technology—while our suicide rates, divorce rates, and crime rates are higher than most nations.

It is never beneficial to be consumed with the spiritual world, but to ignore its reality is certainly not a good idea either. This is one of the things Jesus had in mind when he said the kingdom belongs to little children (Matt. 19:14).

The spiritual world is not just a first-century or third-world phenomenon. Scripture tells us that there is an opposing kingdom to God's (Luke 11:14–23) and that its ruler's intent is to deceive and enslave humanity (2 Tim. 2:26). Evil spirits are assigned to deceive and wreak havoc in the lives of people. Cases of demonization or "possession" are described in Scripture, although they are not behind most of life's issues. Most of our victories and defeats take place on the same battleground: our spiritual thought life. While prayer is crucial and prayerlessness is the epitome of pride, there are some things we must take responsibility for as we inherit our promise.

Ephesians 6:10–18 tells us to put on the whole armor of God. If we put it on in part, we are vulnerable. If we don't put it on, we are vulnerable. Three of the pieces of armor (the breastplate of righteousness, the shield of faith, and the helmet of salvation) we already have when we walk through the door of salvation. Everything else we are to take up, put on, and use. A lot of this is related to not only what we think but how we think. We are to take every thought captive and align it with the person of Christ (2 Cor. 10:5). Notice it says "every thought," not "every thought you think is not from your inheritance in Christ." Deception is deceptive. Some of the things that get in the way of our spiritual inheritance, once we are in Christ, appear to be good and do not always equate to something overtly evil.

Ephesians 6:12 says, "We do not wrestle against flesh and blood, but against the rulers, against the authorities, against the cosmic powers over this present darkness, against the spiritual forces of evil in the heavenly places." There is some sort of structure that has a leader named Satan (Rev. 12:9), who is described as the serpent in Genesis 3. This ruler was personally involved in trying not to assassinate or abduct Jesus of Nazareth but to deceive and tempt him. The same strategy exists for you and me today. Like Jesus came under spiritual assault, we can too. When this happens, it isn't necessarily because we did something wrong. We can, also like Jesus, submit to God, resist the evil one, and emerge in victory.

For this reason, we do well to remind ourselves that "the weapons of our warfare are not of the flesh but have divine power to destroy strongholds" (2 Cor. 10:4). Everyone saved by Jesus Christ is given keys to unlock the right doors. We are also given keys to close and lock those doors that have nothing to do with God's purpose (Matt. 16:19; Rev. 1:18). This means the enemy of our soul cannot force us to do anything, nor are we destined to struggle in life. We can be truly free.

I meet many Christians who commit themselves to chase after God but, when they encounter opposition, become discouraged and quit. Satan is not the opposite of God. As a created being, our spiritual enemy is already defeated (1 John 3:8). How then, if we have the keys we need, the authority of Christ (Luke 10:19), and a defeated enemy, does the evil one still distract so many from their sacred chase? I suggest Mark 5:10–12 provides some clues and, if we will lean into this truth, also provides a solution.

Zero Tolerance

It is worth slowing down and looking closely at this part of Legion's story. In Mark 5:8, it is evident Jesus is speaking to one evil spirit who represents the multitude of spirits. Jesus then asks the man what his name is in verse 9. Verses 10–12 say, "And he begged him earnestly not to send them out of the country. Now a great herd of pigs was feeding there on the hillside, and they begged him, saying, 'Send us to the pigs; let us enter them.'" Some scholars say in verse 10 it appears that the man is the one who begs Jesus not to send the demons out of the country. One can only speculate that, if this is true, the man was so used to his pain and torment he would believe it to be a better alternative than being left alone with those who could merely bind or tame him. Other scholars tell us that it is one spiritual voice, representing the multitude, that asks Jesus not to send them out of the region. What is significant here is the fact that there is a repeated exchange of words and begging, and it all relates to one concept: the demons don't want to leave. Because Jesus is near, and the man is surrendered and wants to be free, they have to. They negotiate in order to not go far away.

There is evidence in Scripture that evil spirits can be stationed at or become comfortable residing in particular locations. For example, Daniel 10:13 describes an encounter an angel has with a demon that is identified by its geographic assignment. There is certainly a structure within the spiritual world (Eph. 1:21; 6:12). Although it is possible the evil spirits don't want to lose their assignment or operate outside of their structure, there is also evidence in the Bible that demons are really not interested in or even capable of having a conscience like this as it relates to authority (2 Pet. 2:4). If they were not interested in keeping under the authority of God in heaven, certainly now that they are depraved and wicked, they care even less.

The legion of demons don't want to leave the country for a deeper reason. The Decapolis, of which Gadara was a part, was described this way by one of its poets: "beloved by demons because full of Hellenizing apostate Jews."[1] Although gentile territory, it appears there was a group of Jews who migrated there. This would have been highly unusual, and even sinful, for a follower of the Jewish faith. Devout Jews would not have intentionally chosen to live in a ceremonially unclean area like this. The dead bodies in the caves and nearby pig herds were an assault on their core religious beliefs, and Gadara had a reputation also of being a site for pagan worship. This is why the poet would say this area was "beloved by demons." People who openly worshiped at pagan shrines, combined with the apostate Jews who knew God in their heads but not in their hearts, made the evil spirits feel welcomed. The demons begged not to remain in the man but to remain in the country because they felt at home where paganism and religious performance cohabitated.

Matthew 12:45 describes the activity of an evil spirit when it leaves a person: "Then it goes and brings with it seven other

136

spirits more evil than itself, and they enter and dwell there, and the last state of that person is worse than the first. So also will it be with this evil generation." If Jesus had complied and simply sent the demons out of the man with nowhere to go, they would certainly have come back to torment the man, and his condition would only have worsened.

We see in the heart of Jesus a desire not to provide temporary relief but total liberation to the man. Jesus doesn't tolerate anything that falls short of God's best for us. Jesus didn't leave the door open for the man's torment, pain, shame, and soul imprisonment to return. Why should we do the same when we justify our compromises or tolerate the counterfeit of our spiritual enemy? One clue left for us in Mark 5:10–12 is this: we don't have to tolerate anything less than God's promise in our lives. We don't need to get used to our past tormenting us and our shame inhibiting us. These lies do not need to—nor do they get to—stay in the "country."

I wonder how many times we come to Jesus and ask him to help us but, deep down inside, we still have those areas that tolerate dysfunction. For example, we ask God to forgive us for our sins but make excuses for our bad temper and call it a weakness. After all, that was just how we were raised, right? We can embrace the reality of living in heaven after we die only to fall short of what our inheritance is in this life. When we set aside all of the excuses to come to Christ for salvation, let's make sure we don't make excuses to begin settling for the very things Jesus came to give us freedom from.

The demons begged to stay in the country because there is nothing more dangerous to the powers of darkness and nothing more irresistible to God than us bending our heart toward God's face with no other voices distracting us. They wanted to stay close to the man to talk him out of who he truly was in Christ, just like the devil tried to do with Jesus in Matthew 4. Jesus would not have it. He was and is the One who knows they always come back seven times stronger. The evil spirits knew they couldn't barter with Jesus. They switched from begging not to leave the country to begging to enter into the pigs that were nestled on the hillside. Jesus permitted them to enter the swine. In doing so, Jesus extends to us another truth we need to embrace: there may be some habits, patterns, or ways of thinking that we need to change in order to inherit what God has promised.

Deviled Ham and Fleas

As a dad of two daughters, I have officially accepted my responsibility to share cheesy dad jokes. For quite a long time this was a daily occurrence at the dinner table. Now that they are young women, my lack of originality is catching up to me. In search of fresh material, I visit websites, joke apps, and find other cheesy dads to further develop my arsenal. But I am running out of material, and am reduced to such gems as: "I once heard someone say that Mark 5, when Jesus drove the demons into the pigs, was 'the beginning of deviled ham.'"

I grew up on deviled ham sandwiches. If you don't know what deviled ham is, just imagine a small can of minced meat and lard. That's about right. We spread a little mustard on white bread, smeared on the canned concoction, threw the sandwiches into brown paper bags, and took them fishing, to the park, and to the basketball court. You may not be inclined to try a deviled ham sandwich after reading that description, but perhaps you're wondering about the sensationalism of this detail in the story found in Mark. Why in the world would Jesus send demons into a herd of pigs? In this remarkable detail, Jesus is shattering artificial hope in religious performance and also taking the lid off the faith of everyone who will experience the man's transformation. What do I mean?

Let's pause and consider the common flea. (No, this is not another dad joke.) Fleas are annoying on household pets, but in the grand scheme of life, they are fascinating little creatures.[2] They can pull one hundred and sixty *thousand* times their own weight. To put that into perspective, it would be like you putting thousands of two-hundred-pound baby elephants on your back and walking. Fleas don't have ears and basically can't see much. They lay up to fifteen hundred eggs in their lifetime. Female fleas are larger than males. They can be frozen for up to a year and revive themselves.

Although there are numerous facts like these about fleas that only a handful of folks like me find fascinating, there is one additional tidbit of information I think you will find interesting—especially since we are talking about intimacy with God: fleas can jump. They can jump thirty thousand times without stopping. And each time they jump, by the way, they reverse directions. With the average flea measuring a mere two to three millimeters, they jump with an acceleration that is fifty times faster than a space shuttle. They jump over one hundred and fifty times their own size, which would be like you jumping from one end zone to another on a football field.

But with what seems to be unlimited potential in how far a flea can soar, there is a rather simple way to limit even the most athletic of fleas. A retired schoolteacher named John Taylor Gatto[3] used a well-known experiment with fleas to explain how our perspective and exposure to things can actually prevent us from reaching our potential. He described a scientist who placed fleas inside of a glass jar. As we have learned, the fleas were able to jump well beyond the walls of the jar and quickly spilled out. Then the fleas were scooped up and placed back in the jar, but this time a lid was placed on top. Boing. Boing. Boing. Ouch. Ouch. Ouch. The fleas jumped up and down and hit their heads on the lid of the jar. After a short period of time, the fleas, although almost completely blind, began to jump with a preciseness that caused their little bodies to hover just below the lid. After the scientist removed the lid, the fleas, though capable of jumping much higher, never went beyond where they had been conditioned to go.

Shame, religious performance, inauthenticity, and refusing to be vulnerable with God can condition us to settle for so much less than what we were designed for. The herd of pigs the demons were sent into by Jesus represented the "lid" the entire area was used to. In this part of the story in Mark 5, Jesus has the longest interaction with an evil spirit recorded anywhere in Scripture. Jesus permitted it to be so. Matthew's account of this story, written for a Jewish audience, draws attention to Jesus and his statement in Matthew 5:17, where the Lord said he didn't come to get rid of the law of Moses but to fulfill it. Eating pork was prohibited in the writings of Moses (Lev. 11:7; Deut. 14:8).

For a herd of swine to run into a lake and drown was not seen at all as a waste of money to a Jew, for they would never have been seen around a pig. Mark is written not for a Jewish audience but for a Roman one. Gadara, a city influenced by the Greeks but under Roman rule, had plenty of swine nearby, partially because Romans used pigs to make sacrifices to their gods, especially for the atonement of their souls.

To the Jewish disciples who were with Jesus, involving pigs in a miracle would have been unconventional and offensive. But the gentiles and casually Jewish people who inhabited Gadara, the Roman soldiers, and the man called Legion who begged Jesus not to send them far away experienced something else. Sending the evil spirits into the pigs signified that some of the things they used to put their hope in, which prevented them from experiencing true freedom, now must be surrendered to the greater way found in Christ.

This detail is included in the story because it is very important. We were created for connection with God and, though the connection was destroyed in Genesis 3, Jesus makes it possible to be spiritually alive and discover how vast God's love for us really is. We have all accumulated baggage, made excuses, been distracted by the lies of the enemy of our soul, and even been seduced by opportunities. The man who encountered Jesus on the shore in Mark 5 summons all of us to lay it all down and respond to our inner yearning for a deeper connection with God.

We start by vulnerably and authentically being who we are before God. We see that our sacred chase has nothing to do with striving or performing. It is from a place of rest in our identity as sons and daughters that we begin to know what is unknowable: God's love for us. Jesus was not repulsed by the tormented man, nor is God ever embarrassed by you. Jesus sent the demons into the herd of swine to demonstrate how the man's sacred chase can continue, and it was found in one word: *surrender.*

Surrender It All

Surrender isn't always easy, but in the life God designed us to inherit in Christ, it is essential. We do not inherit God's good promises by striving and wrestling with our enemy. We are not supposed to become better experts at the way evil works. Romans 16:19 says, "Be wise as to what is good and innocent as to what is evil." Our best strategy to overcome the inferior life isn't to ignore the reality of our spiritual enemy, but we must guard against becoming preoccupied by it.

God is and always should be our focus. It was with one glance at Jesus that the man overcame the torment of thousands of evil spirits. This is a pattern worth adopting. We do not even experience the fuller life by resisting sin and temptation alone. This is necessary, for God's goodness demands our utmost devotion to Scripture, and grace is not our opportunity to presume on God's love. But we are first to submit to God and then resist the evil one, and we will then see freedom come to our souls (James 4:7). We fix our eyes not on the problem but on Jesus.

The sacred chase is paved with surrender, but the reward is beyond worth it. As I seek more of God's reality in my life, I'm learning how to win the battles in my soul, not through fighting but by surrendering. For example, surrender means as a spouse you may need to fight more to connect with your spouse than to be right or make him or her more like you. Surrender looks like confronting your insecurities and being comfortable with who God formed you to be rather than being a chameleon at work to fit in with others. You surrender when you pick up your Bible and read until your heart softens and peace comes once again. Surrender means you don't commit idolatry by changing your definition of who God is to justify the decisions you are or are not making.

Surrender comes in multiple forms, but its substance is always the same. Jesus summed it up this way: "Nevertheless, not my will, but yours, be done" (Luke 22:42). It is about letting go, for then and only then do we truly receive.

Sometimes the idea of being alone frightens us because we need to deal with who we truly are. This may be why we tolerate travelers, like David did, because being alone is too hard. But we are never truly alone. God never leaves us, and he promised to never, ever forsake us. Ester Buchholz said, "Others inspire us, information feeds us, practice improves our performance, but we need quiet time to figure things out, to emerge with new discoveries, to unearth original answers."[4] Learning to hear God's voice in the midst of many others requires more than listening. It requires surrender.

One glance at Jesus is where the sacred chase begins. And it continues by our drawing a line in the sand between us and the distractions or "swine" that used to make settling so convenient and saying they are no longer welcome in our "country." What do you need to change in order to inherit what God has promised? You, and only you, can ultimately let go of it all and run your own race toward God. Yet you run not alone, for God comes, even if you fall, to help you finish.

Sometimes, when our lives appear put together, we stop progressing and pretend that we do not have memories, relationships, spiritual strongholds, thought patterns, beliefs, or behaviors that profoundly shape our intimacy with God. When Jesus, the Light of the World, comes, he exposes those things traveling with us that have found safe haven in the dark corners of our soul. When we are aware, we can respond. When we respond, we can overcome. When we overcome, we inherit another portion of God's kingdom in our lives.

The Crooked Places

The sacred chase often reveals the multiple layers of healing our soul needs. Salvation is based on what Jesus did on the cross. Spiritually, we move from death to life. Our soul, which is our mind, will, and emotions, will continue to undergo renewal and restoration. God lovingly points things out to us, not to shame us but to call us to a higher place of living by expanding our capacity.

In Luke 2:40, we are told that the child Jesus "grew and became strong, filled with wisdom. And the favor of God was upon him." At the age of twelve, Jesus and his parents went to Jerusalem, where Jesus engaged religious leaders in a conversation. They were amazed. "And Jesus increased in wisdom and in stature and in favor with God and man" (v. 52). Jesus was full of wisdom in verse 40 but increased in wisdom in verse 52. How do we grow in something we are full of? We get a larger cup by being faithful with where we are. After all, it was Jesus who said if we are faithful in little things, more will be given (Luke 16:10).

We increase our capacity to inherit a greater dimension of God's kingdom in our lives in a variety of ways. One of them is our willingness and ability to stop making excuses and receive correction from God. If you're a parent, or have ever watched someone raise a child, you've experienced what it is like to tell the child no at one point or another.

Your four-year-old asks, "Can I have another donut?" "No, not now, sweetie," you respond. "It's 9:00 p.m." Your ten-year-old asks, "Can I stay the night with some friends?" You respond, "No, their parents are out of town." Your fourteen-year-old offers to run to the store for you and get some more milk, and you say, "No, you don't have a driver's license." Sometimes *no* is a good word, especially when the parent has the best interest of the child at heart. There are times God says no, and it is for our good as well. For every time God says no, there is an even greater yes we are being invited into. Saying no to sins, transgressions, and iniquities is actually saying yes to God's best.

Psalm 32:5 says, "I acknowledged my sin to you, and I did not cover my iniquity; I said, 'I will confess my transgressions to the LORD,' and you forgave the iniquity of my sin." Though "sin," "iniquity," and "transgressions" all refer to a similar reality, there are some differences between the terms.

The word *sin* means "to miss the mark," and can literally be translated "crouching beast."[5] It is an archery term that serves as a metaphor for aiming toward a bull's-eye but our arrow lands outside of the red circle in the middle. A sin can be something we do that falls short of God's best (Exod. 10:16; Gal. 5:17), like cheating on our taxes. It can also be something we don't do that we should (James 4:17), like caring for the poor and being generous and compassionate. It is also an attitude or thought (Matt. 5:27–30), like lusting after someone sexually or holding bitterness in our hearts.

Transgressions are blatant, intentional sins that violate God's stated standards in Scripture. This is when adultery is chosen by a spouse, a family is abandoned, or an automobile is stolen. When we repent and come to God we can also be forgiven (Ps. 32:1). Iniquities, however, are something a bit deeper. This refers to areas of our soul where we believed a lie and developed a habit, and now, at times through our premeditated choices,

145

harden our hearts toward God in areas where we no longer give him access (1 Sam. 3:13–14; Ezek. 28:15). An example of this is when a workaholic sacrifices time with his or her family and makes excuses because that's the way he or she was raised. People think the individual is a hard worker when in reality he or she simply doesn't know how to rest and be at peace. It is subtle and often difficult to detect. Something is just slightly off deep down inside.

Jesus was wounded for our transgressions because "without the shedding of blood there is no forgiveness of sins" (Heb. 9:22). Our iniquities were initially dealt with not just by Jesus shedding his blood but by Jesus being bruised (Isa. 53:5). In essence, Jesus experienced pain below the surface so we could experience healing in the same way.

Iniquity literally means "crooked."[6] Think of it this way: there are ways of thinking, feeling, and behaving that may seem right to us, because of our experience, but when they are compared to the plumb line of God's best, they are off. When these are not dealt with, we run with all of our might only to feel like we are running in circles. Sometimes we are.

When we don't make the progress we want to see, we can become discouraged, ashamed, feel like other people are much more spiritual than we are, or that God has his favorites and we are not one of them. We certainly shouldn't use God's grace as an excuse to be spiritually lazy. We should also realize it isn't just about trying harder. We were created to pursue God with our whole heart, but pursuit on a crooked path only leads to frustration. Jesus can make our crooked paths straight (Isa. 45:2).

Iniquities must be dealt with if we are to inherit the promises of God in all areas of our lives. The traveler studies your iniquities well. There are things that have accompanied you in life that have become normal, and now, by coming to Christ with them, you can deal with them once and for all.

However, you and I will never reach a place with God where we are too good, too religious, or too Christian to need a course correction every once in a while. Indeed, keeping our hearts open before God to deal with the iniquities will not only prevent disasters like the ones that occurred in David's life but also serve as a sign of humility and love for God.

When Pete said, "It was too hard to let them go," he was acknowledging that sometimes what is familiar, though inferior, becomes our normal. His words also reveal how deep within us there can be crooked places that, over time, take us far off course. Salvation is free and not by our own merit. Our spiritual inheritance takes an entire lifetime to discover, with the help of the Holy Spirit, one intentional and surrendered step at a time.

CHAPTER EIGHT

The Dove Remains

Can you imagine being homeless? Mehran Karimi Nasseri didn't have to imagine.[1] He lived it. Known by some as the "terminal man" and others as "Sir Alfred," he spent more than eighteen years living at Charles de Gaulle Airport in Paris, France. I have been to that airport and know exactly where to go if you want a fresh croissant and a really good cup of French roast coffee. I have no idea where to go if you're going to live there—for eighteen years. Sir Alfred went to Terminal 1.

He was born in Iran in 1943 and was raised by people he thought were his parents. But after his father died, his mother informed him she was not his biological mom. A British nurse was. The family wanted Sir Alfred to move and offered to pay for his university studies in England. His relationship with his family was strained, and he went. When he returned to Iran, he found himself arrested for being an activist. Rather than being sent to jail, he was banished from the country and his passport was only valid for one year. Though this was devastating, you would think that one year should be plenty of time to find a new life.

But not only was he homeless, he was also without a country, or "stateless." In 1988, while in France, he was mugged on his way to catch a flight to England. Without his passport, his disembarkation in London didn't work out well. Without the correct documentation, he was sent back to Paris, where he was arrested for illegal immigration and sent to jail. Six months later, when he had been released, he tried to get permission for entry into other countries, but to no avail. He was afraid to leave the airport and potentially go back to jail, so he found a home on a red bench and, year after year, lived in Terminal 1. People who worked there became fond of him. He ate at McDonald's, lived off of food and cash people gave him, and cleaned up in the restroom. His clothes were sent to the airport dry cleaner. He received letters and donations, and a human rights lawyer from France fought for him and his seemingly most unbelievable predicament. His story caught the attention of media around the world.[2] Steven Spielberg was so inspired by the story he made a movie. In 2006, Nasseri was hospitalized and, upon his release in 2007, he eventually found freedom in the suburbs of Paris in 2008.

Eighteen years is a long time to be homeless not because you are incapable or unwise but are stuck in a system that simply can't fix itself. I can't imagine how it feels to be without a home, constantly unsettled, year after year.

When we surrender to Jesus, not only do we have an eternal home personally prepared for us by Jesus (John 14:3), but we literally become the home where the Holy Spirit lives (1 Cor. 6:19). That's pretty remarkable and mind-blowing. We don't deserve for God to live within us. Yet the Holy Spirit comes and comfortably settles in. Why? We are God's sons and daughters and, according to Isaiah 56:3–5, we also carry "a name better than sons and daughters . . . an everlasting name that shall not be cut off" (v. 5). This is how complete the work of Jesus is on the cross and how powerful our surrender to God is. Like I have heard my wife, Ali, say, you are "God's favorite place to be." God feels at home with you.

I want to make sure I live my life and cultivate my heart in such a way that God always feels welcomed, invited, and like I want him around.

It wasn't for eighteen years, like Sir Alfred, but for thousands of years that the Spirit of God was looking for a home inside each one of God's children. His chosen people were stuck in a system often paralyzed by unbelief, false assumptions, religious abuse, and corruption, and the Holy Spirit looked far and wide to find a place to settle.

Then, in a small, obscure river settlement, one day a small crowd gathered to publicly demonstrate their commitment to God. A gentleman who was rumored to be the product of an extramarital affair and had grown up in a lower-middle-class home stood among them. In an age and place where identity was associated with one's father, he was never referred to as "Jesus, the son of Joseph"; rather, he was always "Jesus, the son of Mary." There is a tradition that Joseph died during Jesus's anonymous years, but this name is also indicative that Jesus never fully escaped the controversy of the virgin birth.

His cousin, John the Baptist, performed the ritual of water baptism on many people that day. Jesus was one of them. When Jesus came up out of the water, he was addressed not by an earthly mother or father but by the heavenly Father.

And when Jesus was baptized, immediately he went up from the water, and behold, the heavens were opened to him, and he saw the Spirit of God descending like a dove and coming to rest on him; and behold, a voice from heaven said, "This is my beloved Son, with whom I am well pleased." (Matt. 3:16–17)

Jesus's identity was solidified by the Father long before Jesus was ever in the public eye and seen as a miracle worker. It is utterly amazing to me that what the Father spoke over Jesus was 100 percent related not to his vocation, education, childhood, or social status, but to his identity.

Our very souls are sustained by God's voice. When you read Scripture, God-breathed words empower you (2 Tim. 3:15–17). When you arise, God sings over you (Zeph. 3:17). When your body needs healing, God has a word for you (Ps. 107:20). Whenever you want to know what God is thinking, just look to Jesus, whose life and message are the perfect representation of the Father's heart. Jesus is literally Scripture in human form (John 1:1, 14). God will always have something to say to you through Scripture, and he will never, ever contradict what is already written in the sixty-six books we call the Bible. Deuteronomy 8:3 says, "Man does not live by bread alone, but man lives by every word that comes from the mouth of the LORD." It is crucial to realize we live and find our spiritual sustenance in what God is saying right here and now. The Spirit of God whispers and thunders to us through God's Word. The Spirit speaks to our heart and our conscience and guides us into all truth (John 16:13). There is an inseparable link between God's Word and the Spirit.

————

Hearing the audible voice of God on the riverbank that day was miraculous. But there was another miracle occurring that day we often overlook. What happened? Before the Father spoke identity over Jesus, the Holy Spirit descended like a dove and landed on the Son of God.

Typically, we have reserved this kind of conversation about the Holy Spirit for Pentecostals, charismatics, or mystical Christians. We tend to think how we engage and respond to the Holy Spirit as a difference of lifestyle or expression, or even a difference of opinion. There certainly are theological differences among the church, and they aren't all bad. I'm sure God likes it when people pray random, spontaneous prayers and also finds pleasure when believers read with heartfelt surrender from a book of prayers. There are differences between biblical mandates, community standards, and personal preferences. Differences and diversity are good. Division never is. Ironically, the Person of the Trinity who is deposited inside each Christian to help him or her live the abundant life is often at the center of much controversy.

Some people have experienced what I would call spiritual abuse. This is when God is used as an excuse to manipulate, pressure, or cause someone to conform. This can happen when someone incorrectly uses Scripture or, unfortunately, even takes the Bible out of context to mean something it never meant. A common error is for a well-meaning follower of Christ to turn a bit of their heart off to the Spirit of God because of a bad religious experience. But using someone else's spiritual immaturity as a reason to turn away from the Spirit of God and what the Bible tells us about him only testifies to our own spiritual immaturity.

Others may be new to the Christian life or grew up in a denominational background where the grace of Jesus was talked about but the Spirit was never mentioned. Sometimes we become critical of what we simply do not understand. The solution is to go to the Bible and see how important the Spirit's work is and should be in our lives, families, and communities. The Holy Spirit is not friendly to some denominations or belief systems and unfriendly to others. The Holy Spirit is not French, Spanish, American, or Russian. The Holy Spirit is God, and he wants to get to know you. If we say we walk with Jesus and are thankful for his death on the cross, and we believe God the Father is good and merciful, but we are not surrendered to the work of the Holy Spirit in our lives, we're missing much of who God is. That would be like taking a large part of your marriage, your paycheck, or your car away and pretending like it doesn't really matter.

Regardless of where you are in your spiritual life, the Holy Spirit is applicable to you because the Spirit is necessary to experience a full and holistic Christian life. God the Spirit enables and empowers us to do exactly what God has invited us to do and to become who God created us to be. In other words, you can't live a healthy Christian life apart from the Spirit. You won't accept the invitation to go on the sacred chase apart from him. In fact, you can't even understand the Bible when you read it, repent of your sins, or make wise decisions without the Spirit of God. The supernatural lifestyle of loving your enemies and overlooking offense requires much more than willpower. The Spirit of God makes the supernatural natural. I pray these words do whatever needs to happen to invite you into a deeper intimacy with Jesus through his Holy Spirit.

We are first introduced to the Spirit of God, or the "dove," in Genesis 1:1–2, on the first page of the first book in the Bible.

What was the Spirit doing?

The Bible says he was hovering over the deep, dark chaos right before God spoke the universe into existence. The Spirit is at peace when you and I would be anxious and even terrified. Why would God's Spirit come live inside of us? God wanted to make peace and creativity accessible to us even when chaos surrounds us. This is how Jesus slept in the bottom of the boat in Mark 4 in the middle of a violent storm. The same Spirit who hovered over chaos was with Jesus. The same is true for us.

Exodus 31:1–4 tells us God filled not a preacher nor miracle worker but an artist with the Holy Spirit. The most creative Person in the world, the Spirit of God, lives inside of each Christian. There are creative solutions available to improve your marriage, increase the effectiveness of your parenting, strengthen your financial future, bring healing to your strained relationships, and cause you to excel in your work—because of the Spirit. Judges 6:34 tells us that "the Spirit of the LORD clothed Gideon, and he sounded the trumpet, and the Abiezrites were called out to follow him." Without the Spirit, Gideon's sound would not have united anyone. As a leader in whom the Spirit of God worked, Gideon was more effective in creating community and providing much-needed clarity to the people. Effective leadership will always find its beginning when someone yields to the wisdom the Spirit of God provides.

The Spirit of God empowered another leader named Saul in 1 Samuel 10:6. The first king of Israel was "turned into another man," and he did something no one had ever attempted before. Unfortunately, the same Spirit who equipped King Saul left him (1 Sam. 16:14) because of his compromised, proud, sinful lifestyle. The Spirit's power can take us places where only deep integrity can keep us.

David knew this well. After he fed the traveler in 2 Samuel 11 and Samuel came to his house a year later, David was forced to stare into the mirror of his own soul and see himself for who he truly was. It was during this time that David recited Psalm 51. What is on the heart of the king who committed adultery and murder, and was now facing the consequences of his sin and iniquity that would reverberate through his family lineage? David was not concerned about his reputation nor losing his throne. David said, "Take not your Holy Spirit from me" (Ps. 51:11). David asked God—in fact, he literally begged God—not to take the Spirit from him. Why? Just like the traveler distracts us from our sacred chase, the Spirit of God is the divine way of keeping us on it.

Joel 2:28 tells of a day when the Spirit of God would not come upon a few select individuals; rather, all genders, ages, and ethnicities would receive the Spirit of God literally "poured out" upon them. The Hebrew word translated "Spirit" in the Old Testament is *ruach*, which, when literally translated, means "wind."[3] This is why, when Jesus was describing the work of the Spirit of God in our lives, he used wind as a metaphor (John 3:8).

I like to think of it this way: if on our sacred chase we envision being on a sailboat, then we must unfold our sail in the right direction. But all of our sailing skills mean nothing unless the wind of heaven, the Spirit of God, catches our sail and drives us forward. Regardless of denominational background or lack of it, the Spirit of God and the great work he does in our lives are accessible to all. Too often we get used to living a partial version of the Christ-centered life, in our own strength, without ever realizing the Spirit's power at work within us. With unlimited spiritual strength available, it is almost humorous to think about the little things that worry us, discourage us, and hold us back.

Baby elephants weigh approximately two hundred pounds when they are born. In the circus, to train them, they are tied to a steel post. Month after month the elephant pulls and tugs without going anywhere. When the elephant is full grown and weighing around sixteen thousand pounds, though it can pull around eight tons of weight, it is still held close to its post with the same rope. What could easily be broken in order to gain true freedom instead serves as a reminder of what normal is. What often holds us back isn't nearly as strong as we think it is.

John 1:32 records the first time in history the Spirit of God descended, or came upon an individual, and never left. This Scripture reveals that, with God, all things are truly possible, for the very Spirit of God can make his home with us. There is no longer a reason to ever allow a "post" to hold us back. For thousands of years, the Spirit came upon people and then left them. When Jesus rose up out of the water after baptism, the dove remained. Jesus is the pattern for our lives. If the Son of God needed the Spirit's work in his life, how much more do we?

One of the miracles that occurred after Jesus died on the cross was the tearing of the curtain in the temple. The purpose of this wasn't just so we could gain access into God's presence but so that the presence of God could be accessible to everyone. Jesus talked about this in John 16 when he made what is arguably, in my opinion, one of the most unbelievable statements I can imagine God saying. He said, "It is to your advantage that I go away, for if I do not go away, the Helper will not come to you. But if I go, I will send him to you" (v. 7). *Now, wait just a minute. It is to our advantage that Jesus leaves us?*

This Can't Be Good

If I had been there, here is where my brain would automatically have gone: *What could be better than being face-to-face with Jesus?* I dare you to find anyone else in all of history who is better to spend time with. Just imagine what it was like to walk with Jesus and all of a sudden watch him feed thousands of people by miraculously multiplying a few loaves and fish!

Everywhere Jesus went, something awesome was bound to happen. Jesus took his friends fishing, and money came out of the fish's mouth! Jesus went up on top of a mountain and started glowing! Every time Jesus spoke it was motivated by love. Jesus was perfect. You could count on Jesus when he made a promise. Jesus knew how to have fun. Jesus was a great listener. My response would have been something like, "No, thank you, Jesus. This can't be good. I am not interested in learning what it's like to walk around with a person called the Spirit who is not you. You're perfect. You're loving. I like your sense of humor. You are God. There is no need for you to leave. Ever."

I can imagine him responding with something like, "Oh, Heath, you have no idea. It is to your advantage that I leave. Once I go, someone else is coming, and if you think living life face-to-face with me is indescribable, just wait and see what life is like when the Spirit comes!"

The Spirit is the Helper Jesus referred to in John 16:7. What's the point of the Spirit working in and through us? It would take volumes of books to write down what we think we know. According to Jesus's own words in John 16, here are some of the things that happen when we have a relationship with the Spirit of God:

- The Spirit of God reveals the difference between right and wrong, real and counterfeit, and always points people in the most excellent way (v. 8).
- The Spirit of God draws people who are spiritually dead, living in sin, and sitting in quiet desperation

toward the heart of a loving Father. This is done not through cheap grace that winks at evil and compromises holy standards but by the truth, which sets people free (v. 9).

- The Spirit of God teaches those in Christ how to live the full life by convicting us of sin and guiding us toward righteousness (v. 10).
- The Spirit of God empowers us to live from a place of victory and freedom, for the enemy of our soul is already defeated (v. 11).
- The Spirit of God is a trustworthy source of truth both for what currently is and for what is to come (v. 13). He takes the inheritance we have in the Father and in Jesus and reveals it to us so it can become our reality (vv. 14–15).

We are never alone or isolated on our sacred chase. The Spirit is always with us. The Holy Spirit's work in our lives is related to God's father-heart. There is power in knowing how the Father looks at us. Of the eight thousand or so promises in Scripture, only one of them is called the *promise of the Father* and, according to Acts 1:5–8, there is power in that promise. The Spirit, who lives within us, cries out constantly, "Abba! [literally, daddy], Father!" (Gal. 4:6). We never have to struggle with the identity we need to embrace if we are to step into our spiritual inheritance. The Spirit tells us twenty-four hours a day, seven days a week, three hundred sixty-five and one-quarter days a year exactly who we are. And what the Spirit cries out deep within us is exactly what Jesus heard on the banks of the Jordan River: *You are my beloved child, and I am well pleased with you.*

Bamboo

The same One who hovered in the beginning as God's purpose emerged, even in the middle of the extreme chaos in Genesis 1:1, is the same One who, by living within us, makes God's best accessible to you and me.

One of the most significant Bible verses in my life is related to the Spirit's work, and it is found in John 3:34: "He gives the Spirit without measure." Who is *he*? Jesus. This is the reason I say we are all as close to God as we want to be. There are no limits to how much we can know the unknowable love of God. Our discoveries never have to end. We are solely responsible for cultivating the spiritual environment we live in.

I am from Iowa and, for this reason, often think in agricultural terms. If the promises of God are like seeds falling on soil, and the Spirit of God is like well-given rain in season, our hearts are the environment. Iowa is known for its agriculture. But if I take rich black soil from Iowa and plant orange seeds from Valencia, Spain, in it, and the rain falls just right, I still won't produce a harvest of oranges.

Why?

The environment is wrong. The right seeds, planted in the right dirt, don't always produce the right harvest. We are responsible to cultivate the environment of our heart so that, by the Spirit of God, we can inherit what God makes accessible to us as sons and daughters by the way we think and the way we live.

Bamboo farmers in southeast Asia understand this.

A strain of rare and valuable bamboo is grown in Malaysia. When the seed is planted in the first year, it is important to water and fertilize as necessary. At the end of the first year, nothing visibly happens. The same process occurs in years two, three, and four. After days of hard work, there are no results observable to the human eye. Four years is a long time to water, fertilize, and stare at the ground hoping something of value will one day grow. The farmer has no guarantees other than that he or she believes that the process will work because, in that particular environment, it has before.

It is in the fifth year that the bamboo grows ninety feet in thirty days.

Just imagine harvesting bamboo in Malaysia and then moving to Alaska, hoping to do the same thing. Four years of work and, in the fifth year, rather than reaping what you've sown, all that grows is disappointment. You can have the right seed and the right soil, and even implement the right process, but without the right environment it won't grow.

This is what happened to Judas Iscariot. He sat around with the other disciples and heard the same teachings, witnessed the same miracles, participated in the same Passover meals, and observed the Sabbath. He produced a different harvest than the others, and it wasn't because Jesus gave him a different type of seed. It is because of the environment of Judas's heart. This is why David prayed in Psalm 51, after the traveler was fed, for God to "renew a *right* Spirit" within him (v. 10, emphasis added). David acknowledged how important the internal reality is to each one of us. What we think, how we feel, our motives, and both the large and microscopic choices that make up our days are the environment the Spirit's work is planted in. When the environment is right, the fruit of the Spirit grows (Gal. 6:9).

We are asked, even commanded, to cultivate a place where the Spirit of God remains. When an individual resists God's

Spirit, he or she fights against God (Isa. 63:10). We are commanded not to grieve the Spirit. In Ephesians 4:30–31 we are then told how this grieving occurs: through our bitterness, anger, slander, and malice. Note that bitterness and malice are in the same verse. We can resist the Spirit of God (Acts 7:51), lie to him (5:3), and insult his grace (Heb. 10:29). We can even quench the Spirit like a flame (1 Thess. 5:19). Hebrews 3:15 is a verse repeated numerous times in the Bible: "Today, if you hear his voice, do not harden your hearts."

When we move from proximity to intimacy, from being almost yielded to being completely authentic and vulnerable with God, paying attention to the subtle whisper of God's Spirit creates the right internal environment for us to spiritually thrive. When we fix our eyes on Jesus, who is the author and finisher of our sacred chase, the same Spirit who landed upon him and empowered him to cultivate a never-ending connection with God lives in us. Romans 8:11 tells us, "The Spirit of him who raised Jesus from the dead dwells in you." Jesus did not have a different Holy Spirit than you do. The same dove who remained on Jesus lives in children, stay-at-home parents, attorneys, PhD physicists, and adolescents. What does it look like in someone's life when the reality of Jesus becomes his or her new normal? The man they called Legion shows us.

Sitting Still

Legion laid aside all excuses and allowed his spiritual hunger to override his struggle. He ran toward Jesus with all of his heart, then stopped and sat down when he encountered the One who is unconditional love (Mark 5:15). A former madman who wore little to no clothing was now fully clothed. The demonized one who didn't even know his real name received a sound mind and a soul at rest (Heb. 4:11). The man felt right at home, at peace, with God. We were created to feel at home with God too. This is why the Spirit of God comes to live inside each of us after we surrender to the lordship of Christ.

Sitting clothed and in our right mind is a great picture of what life can look like when we become intimately connected to Jesus. But according to him, there is something even better in store for us: the Spirit of God comes to us, guides us, and leads us home. After all, our home is a Person, for "in him we live and move and have our being" (Acts 17:28).

When the human soul is planted anywhere other than the presence of God, there is an ever-present sense of disappointment. We were fashioned by and for God to receive a spiritual inheritance in Christ. This is why people who know the gospel and yet do not commit wholeheartedly to pursue him wake up each and every day thinking that something is missing from their life.

To stop moving forward in the kingdom of God is to move backward. Choosing humility, when our pride emerges, keeps our attention on the God-adventure just ahead. Responding in prayer and laying down our burden, before anxiety convinces us otherwise, provides forward motion. Living a life of generosity and selflessness, regardless of the state of the economy, allows the kingdom of God to define our response to the unknown. The kingdom is not stagnant and it does not stay still. The kingdom only advances (Matt. 11:12).

CHAPTER NINE

A New Normal

I never used to wear sunglasses. I thought they were a fashion statement, and I couldn't care less. They were just one more thing to carry, one more thing to try not to forget, and one more thing to purchase. But a few years ago, my eyes started bothering me and seemed to be getting more and more dry and irritated. So I went to the eye doctor, who informed me how important polarized sunglasses would become to me. The doctor saw some spots on my eyes and said that I needed to start protecting them from ultraviolet rays. Within a week of my wearing sunglasses consistently, as needed, my symptoms began to go away. The results were so worth it I even began to take my sunglasses on work trips. They seemed to work just fine until one day, when getting into a rental car to drive to a meeting, I noticed my symptoms returning. This time they were only in my right eye. That seemed odd.

I remember rubbing my eye over and over again. The discomfort from the sunlight coming through the windshield was increasing, and I'd left my eye drops at home. I closed my right eye while driving down the road just to get some relief. It didn't help. I saw a sign for a gas station and pulled off to get some eye drops. My eye remained squinted as I walked into the convenience store and made my purchase. Hopping back into the car, I reclined the seat, opened the eye drops, and took off my sunglasses. I set them on the passenger seat—and that's when, to my astonishment, I was able to self-diagnose the root cause of my irritated and dry eye: I was missing the lens on the right side of my shades.

I had my sunglasses on when I pulled out of the parking garage where the rental cars were. No one said anything. I walked into the convenience store and even held the door open for some customers. Still not a word. The clerk didn't mention my fashion statement either. I felt like a moron. Note: if you ever see someone missing a lens in their sunglasses, please go out of your way to mention it to them. I found the missing lens in my backpack and easily inserted it back into the frame. It's amazing how quickly my right eye recovered once I saw the road ahead through the correct lens. What is interesting to me is that, rather than taking off my sunglasses to check, I just assumed the problem was something different. My solution was to rub my eye and drive down the road with one eye closed.

Sometimes our solution to other life problems is to close our eyes when we simply need to make sure we are looking through the right lens. Those who lived in the region of Gadara closed their eyes too.

The people in the surrounding area were used to the man's screams. They saw him day and night in the limestone caves. They were the ones who worked diligently to bind and tame the man who had become a danger to himself and society. You would think they would high-five Jesus and congratulate the man who had been demon-possessed. There he was, sitting, clothed, and in his right mind—and no one, according to the Scriptures, ran up and hugged him. No one exclaimed how amazing the love of God was.

The evil force inside the man was so strong it caused two thousand swine to run down a steep embankment and drown. Now this man was centered and balanced. Instead of being excited that the naked man was clothed or the tormented man was in his right mind, the people were afraid. That word translated "afraid" is *phobeó* and comes from *phobos*.[1] It is where our word "phobia" comes from. The meaning here is that they didn't just think what happened to the man was creepy or a bit unusual. They were so afraid it can be inferred that their mental state would suffer long-term effects.

What is "normal" is relative. Eskimos think frigid cold is normal and firefighters think extreme heat is. How is "normal" redefined when someone meets Jesus? Jesus becomes the new normal. The people of Gadara were so far from what normal should and could look like that they could handle Legion's pain and torment better than they could his transformation.

They were missing a lens and didn't know it. They were used to seeing reality with one eye closed, and what they thought was the problem was not, at all, the problem. Not only did the demons beg Jesus to leave them be but the townspeople did as well. You would think they would beg him to stick around, but it was quite the opposite. They pleaded with Jesus to leave their region.

And Jesus did.

Knees and Confessions

When the man saw Jesus in the distance at the beginning of Mark 5, he had no guarantees of how God would respond to him. He took a risk, became vulnerable, laid aside all excuses and shame, and pursued Jesus. Surely seeing the effect of one encounter with Christ would make it much easier, even convenient, for the townspeople to embark on their own sacred chase. They witnessed firsthand the effects of meeting Jesus. They saw the freedom any of us can experience when we come to and are transformed by God's mercy. The same invitation that we all have was extended to them—and they refused it. They refused him.

We can see in the story that what made them uncomfortable wasn't just the man's changed life but the destruction of the swine. Although the swine represented everything that should not be in their lives (like pagan worship and moral compromise), the new normal Jesus introduced them to seemed to be too high a price to pay.

We all like talking about Jesus Christ our Savior. Who doesn't want to be saved from eternal separation from God? Who wouldn't want to be literally "saved" from what his or her sins earn them? If I were to ask one million people if they wanted God to save them from heartache and pain, I have a feeling one million people would say yes.

Scripture tells us, however, that not every knee will bow nor every tongue confess that Jesus Christ is "Savior." No, every single knee will bow and every tongue declare that he is "Lord" (Phil. 2:10–11). To view Jesus as Savior but remain unwilling to yield to his lordship is just like Judas calling Jesus his *rabbi*.

The sacred chase is paved with our surrender to Christ's lordship. Salvation is a free gift from God. Jesus already paid the price in full. On the other side of salvation's door, however, our free inheritance emerges on our spiritual pursuit. We must be like the blind beggars on the Jericho road who caught Jesus's attention not because of their condition but because of their passion.

I wonder how often Jesus invites us to another level of our spiritual inheritance but we refuse it and plead with him to leave our presence because it just costs us too much. Oh, we would never admit that. It sounds particularly ridiculous to say God deserves anything less than all of our heart. The reality, though, is that when our hearts are not yielded to the Spirit's whisper, and we resist, quench, or grieve the Spirit's work in our soul, we in essence do the very thing the people of Gadara did to Jesus.

Does Jesus have your permission to access everything and anything in your life if he so chooses?

Amy Carmichael was born into a wealthy family in Ireland.[2] Their wealth quickly disappeared when her father became ill and died. She grew up feeling helpless and, after intimately connecting with Jesus, committed her life to helping those who were in a similar state. Amy arrived in India in 1895, and she invested fifty years of her life there as a missionary. She primarily served many vulnerable and marginalized children. Amy once said, "To any whom the Hand Divine is beckoning: count the cost, for He tells us to, but take your slate to the foot of the cross and add up the figures there."[3]

When speaking about the lifestyle of intimacy with God and the temporary distractions in this life, she said, "We profess to be strangers and pilgrims, seeking after a country of our own, yet we settle down in the most un-stranger-like fashion, exactly as if we were quite at home and meant to stay as long as we could. I don't wonder apostolic miracles have died. Apostolic living certainly has."[4]

Amy saw a difference between proximity to God and intimacy with God. When every knee bows and every tongue confesses that Jesus Christ is Lord, may it be said of you and me that we did so voluntarily while we still had breath in our lungs. Hopefully, our primary motivation isn't just so we can go to heaven after we die but so that all of heaven, which is our inheritance in Jesus, could become our reality here on earth.

The Thirteenth Disciple

Saying no to the sacred chase is not something unique to the people of Gadara and Judas Iscariot. In Matthew 19:16–22, we read another story of a follower of Jesus who allowed a lack of lordship to get in the way of intimacy with God. The story goes like this: A young man addressed Jesus not as Lord but as teacher (literally, *rabbi*) with his question: "Teacher, what good thing must I do to get eternal life?" (v. 16 NIV). Jesus, of course, responded by asking another question: "Why do you ask me about what is good? There is only One who is good" (v. 17 NIV). But then he gave the young man the list he was asking for: honor your father and mother, love your neighbor, don't commit adultery, and so on. Nothing on this list was new for this young man. He had likely memorized much if not all of the Old Testament, as was common for Jewish men in the first century.

So the young man then said to Jesus, "All these I have kept" (v. 20), and Jesus's response here is perfect—his response always is. He told the young man that there was one more thing he needed to do: sell everything he owned, give it away to the poor, and come follow him. Scripture says the young man "went away sad, because he had great wealth" (v. 22 NIV). Usually, what sabotages our passionate pursuit and deeper connection with God is something that causes discomfort or inconvenience to us. It is important we remember to hold loosely the very things God has given that we may one day be required to let go.

When Jesus invites the rich young man to "Come, follow me" (v. 21), these specific and significant words can get lost in our modern context. What do they mean?

Rabbis in first-century Judaism personally invited a small, exclusive group of students to devote years of their lives to participate in something similar to an apprenticeship. Each rabbi had what is called a "yoke," which was a set of beliefs and interpretations he sought to teach the next generation. To take a rabbi's "yoke" upon you meant you were committing to learn and represent that rabbi's particular way of seeing God and the world. This is why Jesus said to take his yoke and make it ours (Matt. 11:29).

The words Jesus spoke to the young man were not welcome. They were an inconvenience, and this exposed the young man's heart for what it was. This moment with the Lord was special, life-altering, and certainly not something that made the young man feel pressured or disappointed. Make no mistake: there must have been a strong sense of conflict in the heart of someone Jesus of Nazareth personally looked in the eyes, invited with the divine voice, and provided an opportunity of a lifetime. He could walk closely with God and glean from the One who was there from the beginning. But he didn't humble himself, and so he missed the opportunity to take advantage of this.

This story is much more than a critique of those who have money or are wealthy. Money is not the root of all evil; the love of money is. Wealth, if stewarded well, can honor God in many ways through acts of generosity and compassion. If we read it this way, we not only miss the point of what Jesus is trying to say but also misinterpret the passage to mean there is a "morality" to money—how much we have or don't have.

Many Christians get stuck in the trap of thinking poverty is more spiritual than riches, which is not the case. The point of the story is not that this man had a lot of property. The point is that he wasn't willing to relinquish his most precious possession to be close to Jesus. Something got in his way. His eyesight was skewed, and rather than discovering why, he simply squinted and got used to it. He adapted to what he thought normal should be.

———————

The new normal Jesus introduced the young man—and all of us—to is about seeing this life through God's eyes. It means we derive value from the permanent things. Significance is found not in doing more but in being present in the moment. When Jesus becomes our new normal, we, like him, are vulnerable enough to weep over the death of our friend, though Lazarus will rise from the dead. We are so full of love that we look our betrayer in the eyes, like Jesus did Judas, and we call him friend. It also means, though we love those who hurt us and refuse to become cynical, we still establish boundaries when necessary. After all, Jesus didn't invite Judas to go everywhere with him. Is it possible for Jesus to be standing right in front of us and we miss him? This story makes it clear it is.

Yes, Jesus will even ride the dangerous wind and waves to come to the shore where you are. Jesus has come as close as he can. We are all as close to God as we want to be. But many of us, like the rich young man, allow things to get in the way. Some people allow sin, compromise, and the world's counterfeit to talk themselves out of what truly matters, which is intimacy with God.

There are other voices equally as cunning and convincing that seek to cheat us out of our inheritance as well, and they don't always appear to be as bad as we would think. We are all one rational excuse away from leaving our inheritance in Christ in this life unclaimed. When God invites you to take the next step on your sacred journey, just say a resounding yes. Shout it! You will never regret it. In the conversation that echoes in eternity, you will never hear the voice of regret for surrendering to Jesus too soon.

For a minute, stop and think about what is most precious to you. My guess is it isn't money (although maybe it is). Chances are it's your spouse, children, reputation, work ethic, relationships, profession, retirement account, or maybe a dream you've been holding on to for years. Maybe, if you're single, the most precious thing in the world to you is the idea that you will someday get married. Perhaps, if you don't have kids, it is the hope of someday being a parent. Maybe it's a job you want or a level of success you hope to achieve.

Whatever it is, these things are not inherently bad, but they can become distractions from our connection with God. For the young ruler with a great deal of land, the idea of letting go of his many assets kept him from following Jesus. For you, it might be something different. Either way, don't miss the sobering reality of this story.

Jesus called this man to be a disciple—and the man missed it because something got in the way. For all this time, the man had been living a good, moral life. He had been making all the right choices. He had been living by his own strength. Jesus gave him the opportunity to surrender to a different kind of reality, to deepen his connection with God by letting go of another earthly distraction, and he missed it. Actually, he rejected it.

This could have been a beautiful new start for this man.

This encounter with Jesus is the last we hear of this man in the entire Bible. We don't know what became of him. We can hope that days, weeks, or years down the road, he took a second look at his decision and maybe even changed his mind. But we can't know for certain.

What we do know is that, while God heals and changes the broken, empty, languid, cheating, lying, and even drunk characters in the Bible to bring heaven's purpose to the earth by his grace, when it comes to the young man who chose his riches over Jesus, he fades ingloriously into history. Just another dying star whose light travels in the sky though it burned out long ago.

We Need More Sheets

The former COO of Ritz-Carlton Hotels, Horst Schulze, told the story of one manager's discovery of a problem that seemed to confuse almost everyone.[5] Numerous complaints came in to management because room service was repeatedly delayed. The eggs were cold, the toast was hard, and guests who counted on prompt delivery were inconvenienced. Mr. Schulze described a typical response in most organizations as being something along the lines of scolding the supervisor for being incompetent and blaming him or her for the complaints. As one could expect, the discouraged supervisor would then gather their staff around and do the same to them. Blame would cascade down from one person to the next. But this isn't what happened at the Ritz-Carlton.

The manager responsible assembled the team, and they studied the problem. The kitchen staff prepared the food on time and placed it on the appropriate trays with lids. The staff quickly took the trays to the elevator for delivery. The issue, they discovered, had nothing to do with the kitchen staff but rather the service elevators were not always available. This delayed delivery. Then, rather than assuming there was a glitch in the computers or that the elevators needed repair, they continued to study the situation by using a stopwatch to time the elevators for an entire morning. The location, usage, and availability of each of the elevators was logged.

The reason the food was delayed and arriving to the rooms cold had nothing to do with irresponsible kitchen staff or faulty elevators. A decision by management to reduce the number of bedsheets on each floor was causing the housekeepers to use the elevators more frequently, thus tying them up more. Trying to save money by reducing the number of bedsheets purchased, stored, and washed—a good thing for any manager to think of—actually created more challenges in the long run and resulted in disappointed and angry customers and poor room service.

Misdiagnosing a problem never results in solving it.

The sacred chase isn't about setting aside every rational excuse and beginning a journey. It is about killing every single excuse and refusing to allow it to ever have a resurrection. Excuses creep into our lives like an undetectable virus. Behind the stained glass of our religious experience, we can even justify them. We can look around and see the illusion of progress only to discover, like the small hamster on the wheel, that we are running in place.

What we see around us provides us with supposed evidence that we are advancing along with the kingdom of God, but progress isn't always measurable. It is about cultivating a deeper, never-ending connection with God. This should be normal. The young man said yes many times, as is evidenced by the life he lived. But when Jesus summoned him to another yes, it was too inconvenient, and I'm sure his internal rationale for saying no to God this time made all the sense in the world.

One Continuous Yes

On the other side of the door of salvation, our excuses for being content with how far we've come sound just like "I feel unqualified," or "I am unworthy of a greater inheritance in God." We can be too attached to physical possessions or relationships we don't want to lose. What is unknown terrifies us. Those we read about in Scripture had to cultivate a life of saying a continuous yes to God. This is what accepting his lordship means. It is the evidence we are still running our race in such a way as to win the prize—which is not a trophy or reward but a Person.

Nehemiah led the construction efforts in ancient Jerusalem when the wall needed repairs. We have no evidence in Scripture or history that he had training as an architect, project manager, or laborer. His job was to take sips out of the king's cup to ensure there was no poison in it. He basically drank beverages all day and risked his life doing so. He was a glorified servant who didn't live in Jerusalem. But God invited him to take another step on the chase, and he did it. A task that took an enormous team of people, an immeasurable amount of logistical support, and true grit was led by Nehemiah, who would have had no idea what he was doing. His yes to come and follow God to rebuild the wall was enough. God was the Lord over Nehemiah's inadequacies.

An uneducated farmer who'd never seen rain as we know it didn't go to the hardware store and purchase blueprints to build the ark. Noah was told by God that it would rain forty days and nights. I can imagine his neighbors heckling him and criticizing him. If Noah was like you and me, perhaps, even as the ark was coming into reality, deep down inside he wondered what in the world he was doing. Why would God tell him to build an ark? Why couldn't God just pick him and his family up and set them on the world's tallest peak? Little did Noah know that the entire earth would be flooded, and even the tallest peak would be too low. For one hundred and twenty years, Noah told the onlookers of what was to come and only saw a handful of people respond positively to the message. Those who responded were his family, and Noah's yes to come and follow God saved the human race. God was the Lord over Noah's seemingly mundane and unfruitful efforts.

And then there was David, a boy who smelled like sheep. He wasn't trained to be a fighter, for he took on the lowly occupation of shepherding. He delivered sandwiches to the soldiers who were standing on the front lines of the battle when Goliath taunted them all. Not one of the Israelite soldiers stepped up to defend their families and homeland, so God invited this little "nobody" to come and follow him.

David's sacred pursuit didn't take him directly to a palace with a lush lifestyle nor to a place of fortune and fame. God led the young man straight into a conflict without the appropriate weapons to defend himself.

You may have said yes to God and counted the cost but, in the middle of your obedience, realized how God's invitation to follow took you to a place that just didn't match up with what you presumed it would be. Doubt wants to settle in. Discouragement wants to intimidate you. Deception says you made a mistake, and the enemy of your soul says you don't have what it takes to make it. If you feel ill-equipped, take heart. David did too, and rather than fighting in his own strength or putting on King Saul's armor, David remained true to who he was and who God is. He defeated the giant with a shepherd's sling and a few stones he gathered from the river. God was Lord when

David knew what needed to happen but wasn't quite sure exactly what would occur next.

In the New Testament we meet Paul (initially called Saul of Tarsus), who was infamously associated with the persecution of Christians. As a young man he said yes to a rabbi named Gamaliel and studied under one of history's most notorious Jewish teachers. He had a lucrative career ahead of him, and all of the world's accolades to prove it.

In Acts 9, the man who became Paul met Jesus and basically said yes to come and follow him instead. Paul had destroyed many lives and would have had so many regrets. He ended up writing more of the New Testament than any other writer. We know today that in all things God works out a better plan (Rom. 8:28) and is able to do far beyond anything we could ask or imagine (Eph. 3:20) because of Paul's yes. Jesus was Paul's Lord when things seemed to fall apart.

Sadly, we don't know what the young man's yes to Jesus in Matthew 19 produced because that one, simple, three-letter word was never uttered to God.

The ways of this temporary life can train our spiritual eye to see without the right lens. We see in Mark 5 that the man who sat clothed and completely at peace already knew how important a continual yes to God was. After Jesus was begged by the townspeople to leave the region and was on his way out of town, the one whose sacred chase began in a limestone cave in Gadara and took him to the shore asked Jesus if he could go with him. All the man wanted was to be near Jesus.

I think that's a good attitude to have in life. Our desire to be closer to Jesus makes us an even bigger blessing to our spouse, children, and family. When we go to work, by longing to be near to Jesus, we work with excellence and go above and beyond. With so many opinions swirling in the media and city streets, being close to him makes truth accessible and clear.

The man who simply wanted to be near Jesus didn't hear the words "Come and follow me"; instead, Jesus said something that seems terribly cold and insincere. Jesus told the man to "Go home" (Mark 5:19). Sometimes the sacred chase doesn't result in accomplishing a big dream that the world takes notice of. When we run our race swiftly and undeterred, we may cross the finish line and hear the applause not of the crowd but of One.

Living a life of saying a continual yes to Jesus our Lord may mean we have the dream opportunity we long for, like the young Jewish men experienced when they heard their rabbi say, "Come and follow me." We know what happened to the disciples who heard Jesus say these words to them and responded with a yes.

According to church history and tradition, the twelve ordinary men we know as the Lord's apostles added up their figures at the foot of their cross, and all but one gave his life for his faith.[6] Peter was crucified (upside down upon personal request) in Rome around AD 66 at the hand of Emperor Nero. Andrew traveled to what was the former Soviet Union and to modern-day Turkey, and died in Greece, where he was crucified. Thomas is said to have traveled to India, where he died having been pierced with the spears of four soldiers. Philip shared the life and message of Jesus Christ in North Africa and Asia Minor. After the wife of a Roman proconsul became a Christian, the proconsul arrested and killed him. The tax collector named Matthew, whose Gospel we read, served in Persia and Ethiopia. Some say he disappeared while others say he was stabbed to death in Ethiopia.

Bartholomew is credited with ministry in India, Armenia, Ethiopia, and Arabia. Though accounts vary, he died as a martyr. James went to Syria, where we are told by Josephus he was stoned and then clubbed to death. Simon the Zealot was martyred in Persia when he refused to worship the sun god. Matthias, chosen when lots were cast in Acts 1 to replace Judas Iscariot, was burned alive in Syria. James and Thaddeus also gave their lives for the gospel. The only apostle whom tradition says was not martyred is John. Tradition also says he took care of Mary, the mother of Jesus, in his own home, and pastored the church in Ephesus. One particular story tells us he was dipped into a cauldron of boiling oil but survived. He eventually was sent to live as an exile on the island of Patmos, where his experience is documented in the book of Revelation.

The men Jesus invited to come and follow him also wrote books that we read today in our Bibles, watched as entire cities and regions were changed with the gospel, witnessed countless miracles, and are still known to this day. The Gadarene man who was liberated from thousands of excuses as to why he shouldn't begin the sacred pursuit of God never became a well-known figure in church history. We don't even know his name. Why? Jesus simply instructed him to go home. Well, he did so, and his continual yes undoubtedly produced just as much positive change as the disciples' yes did. Your simple yes to begin, continue, and finish your sacred chase will as well.

CHAPTER TEN

Go Home

No one ever regrets his or her continual yes to Jesus. I personally learned how powerful and practical one continual yes can be when I was, quite literally, in the middle of nowhere.

It was the first time I'd ever walked on the side of a volcano. I was with a group, and we were on the long walk to go to a village that had, as we were told, supposedly never encountered a foreigner before nor ever heard the name of Jesus. The sun overhead felt like it was draped over us and the heat made it difficult to breathe. There are times when it is so hot you don't feel the beads of sweat drip down your face. Why? The sweat just evaporates. Each one of us had a backpack full of supplies, including two liters of water, and those who were able also carried a box of Bibles on their shoulders. We walked for hours. By the time we came up and around a bend in the path on the side of the volcano, we were at a place of desperation and needed to stop, find some shade, and rest. But shade was hard to come by, and that's when I saw it. I thought I was hallucinating.

The brown dirt path twisted and turned like a python on the green landscape. Then, up ahead, to my left, I saw a small wooden table beside the road with a little boy dressed in beautiful indigenous clothing standing beside it. He didn't seem surprised when our group came toward him. His table was intentionally placed there, beside a few trees, and he calmly waited for us to approach. But what I thought was a hallucination turned out to be reality. And what else did I see?

Stretched across the road, tied with a tattered piece of rope on each side to trees, was a banner. Not just any banner, but a Coca-Cola banner. And standing on top of the boy's little wooden table were what appeared to be six-ounce bottles of Coke.

My favorite beverage in the world is an ice-cold Coca-Cola in those little glass bottles. Nothing tastes better than a cold Coke on a hot day. I couldn't believe it. As far as the eye could see, there were no buildings, no airplanes painting the sky with jet streams, and I couldn't see another soul except for my team and this young man. Well, the Coke wasn't ice cold, but I did purchase one. Hey, a steaming bottle of Coke is better than nothing when you're parched! How in the world did the Coke delivery person arrive there before the name of Jesus?

I did some research when I made it back to civilization. Call it simple curiosity or sheer genius, but nobody in the history of the world would or could have ever predicted how a pharmacist in Atlanta would leave a mark on history. John Pemberton's brown liquid, mixed with carbonated water, originally sold for five cents a glass. Its name, Coca-Cola, came from a bookkeeper,[1] and after a year of sales the pharmacist had only sold nine glasses of the beverage per day. A few years later, by 1891, a businessman in Atlanta named Asa Griggs Candler had secured the rights to the business. Although the business grew, it struggled, and eventually Candler sold the business to Ernest Woodruff. In 1923, a young man named Robert, Ernest's son, became the president of the small company.[2] Robert ended up investing more than sixty years doing something about his passion for the soft drink.

What started out as nine glasses per day is now approximately 10,450 Coca-Cola branded soft drinks *per second* all over the world. It is the world's largest distributed product, and you can enjoy one in every country of the world except, at the time I write this, Cuba and North Korea.[3] Given the company's history, I am sure even that will change soon. The world's most recognizable term is "okay," followed by "Coca-Cola." That statistic is staggering to me, and, frankly, out of this world. Speaking of out of this world, Coca-Cola was the first soft drink in space. And the next time you look up to the sky and see the sunlight reflecting off the moon, know this: if all the Coca-Cola bottles in the world were laid end to end, they would reach to the moon and back more than 1,677 times.[4]

How did the Coca-Cola name, beverage, logo, and delivery person get to the side of that volcano before the good news of Jesus did? Coca-Cola traces much of its global expansion to a handful of decisions by Robert Woodruff. Two of his most important were creating the six-pack carton and making Coca-Cola available to all US military personnel during World War II. What started as a fountain drink sold in shops and restaurants quickly became something people could take home, thanks to the carton. What was a US phenomenon became a global one after World War II, thanks to the more than sixty bottling plants in North Africa, Europe, and the Pacific the company built to distribute the drink to US soldiers.[5]

Mr. Woodruff's passion for the soft drink and his desire for it to be accessible to everyone, in every moment of life, even during a global conflict like WWII, started something that has been unstoppable. Coca-Cola's name and reach are massive. One consistent passion is how that little iconic bottle of Coca-Cola made it to the side of the volcano and stood there, just waiting for me, disguised as a mere illusion under the hot sun.

What if you allowed your passion for a deep, never-ending connection with God to run wildly constant for the remainder of your life? What if you cultivated a deep desire to know what is unknowable—the love of Christ—and set aside every excuse, no matter how rational and justified it seemed, to let your soul run free toward the One who stands ready to introduce you to the new normal? This is what the sacred chase is all about. We chase, not in striving for God's approval but in abandonment and reckless love after the One who gave it all. Jesus is worthy of our audacious pursuit.

Day after Day

The results of Coca-Cola's passionate yes didn't come overnight. But they did come, just like they did for the man called Legion. He never heard Jesus say to come and follow him; instead, he was instructed to merely go home. This was not a lack of invitation on Jesus's part to the man. Jesus's instruction to go home was all about learning how to daily live naturally supernatural, something we are called to as well. This pursuit, day after day, produces compound interest for our soul when we draw near to God in our thoughts, attitudes, and actions. What we think is ordinary is extraordinary in costume.

There are no ordinary days, for each one of them is hand-crafted by life's great Artisan. Psalm 139:16 says, "Your eyes saw my unformed substance; in your book were written, every one of them, the days that were formed for me, when as yet there was none of them." These days, written by God's own hand for our life, must be inherited. We must do something with them. Psalm 90:12 puts it this way: "Teach us to number our days that we may get a heart of wisdom." Notice that God doesn't solely number our days for us. We are supposed to number them too. Numbering days is not striving; rather, it is stewardship and a posture of heart.

The Hebrew word translated "number" can mean to appoint, count, or assign.[6] It can also mean to count the children, like a schoolteacher would, making sure each and every one of them was back on the bus as the field trip to the zoo wrapped up. I have been responsible for children on trips like that before—both my own and someone else's—and I can assure you nobody who truly feels the weight of the responsibility simply hopes all of the kids get on the bus when it is time to leave. In places like crowded amusement parks, Ali and I always kept a close eye on our kids because we loved them and wanted to keep them safe. This is the word picture the psalmist uses. We are to keep watch over each and every day like we would a child.

There have been days I didn't number because I allowed the anxieties life breeds to become more real than God's love for me. I worried when I should have prayed. Rather than responding, I reacted. I allowed doubt to creep in when God spoke a better word. Countless times, I have given in to life's temporary matters and ignored, yet again, the presence of God's Spirit, who always wants to invite me yet again to inherit what God promised.

We number our "days," or *yom*.[7] This means much more than Sunday morning during church or Tuesday night with some friends. *Yom* can refer to day, night, or periods of time. This word is much more than the way we understand time. Time does not just progress from 8:00 a.m. to 9:00 a.m. Life includes both times and seasons (Eccles. 3), and God is over them all. We number the days we appreciate and enjoy as much as we number the nights when our vision grows dim and we don't always know what will come. We number them—or stop for a moment and make sure our soul is accounted for, just like a schoolteacher would on that field trip—because our days are actually God's days.

In Psalm 90:12 the word translated "teach" makes the entire verse come together like a perfect jigsaw puzzle. The Hebrew is *yada*,[8] and it means much more than using your brain. It is the same word used in Genesis 4:1 when it says, "Now Adam *knew* Eve his wife, and she conceived and bore Cain" (emphasis added). Asking God to teach us how to make the most of each and every day, or "[make] the best use of time" (Eph. 5:16), is much less about plugging the right appointments into our smartphones or making sure our selfies are time-stamped and much more about a heart posture that, with the slightest glance from God in our direction, says, "I just want to *know* you more, God." It is not for the faint of heart. In essence, it is our expression of worship and dependence on God for all things. It is the most practical way to allow the roar of our heart and love for God to echo in the throne room of heaven and resound in the earth.

When Jesus says in Matthew 7:23 that some people will hear from God, "I never *knew* you" (emphasis added), he uses a Greek word that reflects the essence of the Hebrew *yada*.

Perhaps one of the main reasons our multitude of excuses win day after day in our lives is because they make so much sense. That may be the issue. Our inheritance is trapped because of what is in our minds. Can an inheritance really go uninherited because of this?

———

The tragic death of thirty-year-old CEO Gerald Cotton left his family and friends hurting.[9] And it also left about two hundred million dollars uninherited. Cotton was the leader of a digital exchange company, and he took personal responsibility for the funds, coins, banking, and accounting of his five-year-old business. He believed in strong security and took significant steps to avoid being hacked, a real risk within the digital currency space.

But this CEO's efforts were so secure that, when Cotton passed away, no one knew the passwords needed to access the inventory of cryptocurrency. Efforts have to date proved unsuccessful and, with courts and lawsuits involved, I am not sure what has or will happen to that inheritance.

Life in God is lived not with the thinking mind alone but with the thinking and feeling heart (Prov. 23:7) that beats in rhythm with God's. We must access the heart and mind of Jesus, for this is where the "password" to our spiritual inheritance is. This is what spiritual passion is all about.

Sadly, history is full of those who did not number their days. Pharaoh missed his opportunity with God, although God supernaturally demonstrated his power and love over and over again. Jeremiah 46:17 says, "Pharaoh king of Egypt is only a loud noise; he has missed his opportunity" (NIV). You and I have both committed the same mistake Pharaoh made. But we can move forward, refuse to be tethered to that little stake in the ground like the elephants, and commit the rest of God's days that will be lived out through us into divine hands. We can make the most of each and every moment with our sacred pursuit. This is what the man, whose name we do not know, did on the shores of Gadara.

The opportunity he wanted more than anything, to be with Jesus face-to-face (which, by the way, was more than reasonable!), came packaged in a different form: going home. This opportunity may not seem like much to the casual observer, but rather than falling into the same pattern of excuse after excuse, the man seized it and, like Coca-Cola's Robert Woodruff, demonstrated how powerful one consistent passion can be. The Gadarene man who used to make his home among the tombs learned how to make his home with God. Where did God's days take him?

Mark 5:19–20 tells us what happened when the man begged Jesus to let him continue on the same journey with him and his disciples.

> And he did not permit him but said to him, "Go home to your friends and tell them how much the Lord has done for you, and how he has had mercy on you." And he went away and began to proclaim in the Decapolis how much Jesus had done for him, and everyone marveled.

The same people who kicked Jesus out of their region now began to marvel not at what Jesus was saying but at what Jesus was doing in and through the unnamed man. Jesus didn't say, "Go and tell them what an opportunity they missed while I was among them." No, Jesus wanted him to share God's mercy with those who'd rejected him and give them another opportunity. Mercy is when God does not give us what we deserve. I am grateful for mercy.

Interdependent and Intentional

We need God's mercy on our sacred chase, for it is a journey not of independence but of interdependence. Although our passion for a deeper connection to Jesus is a vital ingredient, we cannot do it on our own. It was God's mercy that transformed the man's life and also mercy that sustained him. Jesus gave the townspeople more than one opportunity, just as God does for each of us. If you are breathing right now, and you are, then God's mercy invites you to inherit your spiritual inheritance of knowing, truly *knowing*, God's love day after day after . . . well, it depends on how long you are willing to number them.

When we look at the life of Jesus, our new normal, we see how numbering our days requires being very intentional. Have you ever wondered what Jesus was like as a person who followed God? Yes, Jesus was and is God, but he was also fully human. He demonstrated how to have one ultimate, consistent passion by applying eight basic spiritual choices. This list is not exhaustive, but it provides some practical next steps to help us consistently say yes.

1. Jesus embraced questions. As a preadolescent, Jesus went to Jerusalem with his parents (Luke 2:41–52). Verse 46 says Jesus was "sitting among the teachers, listening to them and asking them questions." There is a difference between opinion and wise counsel. We are instructed in Scripture to learn from trustworthy people who love God. Rather than having a know-it-all attitude, Jesus was open to learning not just in his mind but in his heart. In the New Testament, one of the Greek words for "miracle" is *mysterion*, where we derive our word "mystery."[10] Some of God's greatest miracles are shrouded in mystery, and this is often where our questions come from. Questions are healthy if they lead us to God's face (Prov. 25:2), where we always hear the truth from our trustworthy Lord.

2. Jesus applied truth. Jesus didn't just ask questions but also answered them (Luke 2:47). Jesus, at the age of twelve, astounded and amazed the spiritual teachers of his day. This tells us that we don't necessarily need to be a Christian for decades and have degrees in theology to develop our spiritual intelligence. "Spiritual intelligence" is a phrase I use not to describe the number of Bible verses we know by memory (though this is valuable and important) but to refer to the Bible verses we apply to our lives. If we don't apply what we know, our faith is dead (James 2:20). What does this look like? To start with, we can all live lives with love, joy, peace, patience, kindness, and the rest of the fruit of the Spirit (Gal. 5:22–23). Remember, the more spiritual we are, the more practical we become. Applying truth isn't complicated or a struggle. It is choosing the fruit of the Spirit when it isn't always convenient or popular.

3. Jesus developed a spiritual rhythm. For example, Luke 4:16 tells us Jesus went regularly to the synagogue. He folded into his life moments when he came together with others to worship, pray, hear Scripture taught, and live in community with others who loved God. Going to church is important, but I want you to understand that this verse doesn't just describe Jesus "going to church" but rather weaving spiritual patterns and habits into his life. Rather than waiting until you happen to have time to connect with God, it really helps to deliberately cultivate a pattern. This looks like praying and reading Scripture in the morning, worshiping God on your way to work, reading Scripture at night so your heart meditates on it as you sleep, attending church regularly, and talking about what God is showing you in life with your family and friends. For some reason, people think being intentional and disciplined in spiritual things makes it "religious" or "inauthentic." Well, I'm sure those same people appreciate their employer adhering to the pattern of paying them on time. Being intentional is about as authentic as it gets. It means you and I pursue what matters most.

4. *Jesus prioritized Scripture.* When Jesus was tempted in Matthew 4, his response was to meet the deception and lies of the devil with the truth of Scripture. When you read the words of Jesus in the Gospels, it is evident he knew the Old Testament, which is the Scripture he had access to. When we meditate on God's Word, both the Old and New Testaments, it literally prospers us and makes us successful (Josh. 1:8). The Bible can bring healing to the soul (Ps. 107:20). The Bible is what the Spirit of God often uses to draw us closer to God. The Spirit's voice will never contradict Scripture, and "all Scripture is breathed out by God and profitable for teaching, for reproof, for correction, and for training in righteousness" (2 Tim. 3:16).

5. *Jesus submitted to authority.* For the Son of God to leave heaven and come to earth is remarkable. Jesus didn't show up and tell people what to do. Jesus submitted to the authority of his parents (Luke 2; John 2), the authority of his heavenly Father (Luke 22:42), and earthly authorities (Matt. 22:21). Submitting to authority doesn't mean we do whatever we are told by anyone and everyone. It does mean we are the best employee we can be, we are the best citizen we can be, and we honor whatever authorities are in our lives.

We live in a generation where cynicism seems to rain down and water the earth with toxic thoughts. I wonder how different our world would look if Christians were known as being the most honorable and humble people in their school, work environment, neighborhood, and gym.

6. *Jesus made no excuses.* Jesus could easily adopt the attitude that he didn't need to pray, know the Bible, go to synagogue, or even come to the earth to die for our sins. But Jesus voluntarily laid down his life for us. He voluntarily often withdrew to a place of prayer. He voluntarily went into the synagogue as was his custom. Jesus voluntarily paid taxes. He voluntarily spoke up when it wasn't popular but it was right. There is not one time in the Bible when God ever makes an excuse. This is a pattern worth noticing. Love God and love people, no matter what. In this, we can all grow.

7. *Jesus didn't confuse proximity and intimacy.* In John 5:30 Jesus said, "I can do nothing on my own. As I hear, I judge, and my judgment is just, because I seek not my own will but the will of him who sent me." Jesus spent eternity, before time began, with the Father and the Spirit. When Jesus stepped into time, his experiences before he became a human being on the earth did not replace his ongoing desire to still connect with the Father and the Spirit. The Spirit, descending like a dove, landed and remained. Jesus only said and did what he saw and heard his Father say and do. This is a description not of physical nearness but of spiritual intimacy.

8. *Jesus prayed.* Luke 5:16 says, "Jesus would often go to some place where he could be alone and pray" (CEV). Think about that for a moment. Jesus was, is, and always will be God. Jesus was there at the creation of the world, lived a sinless life, fulfilled the Old Testament law perfectly, raised the dead, and

worked countless miracles. Yet Jesus still "often" prayed. If the Son of God needed to have one passion in one constant direction through prayer, how much more do we! A prayerless person is often a powerless person who becomes a victim of his or her circumstances. Prayerlessness exists in many lives today. If it does in yours, that can change now. You can talk to God in the car, in the grocery store, at work or school, with family and friends, and alone. At the mention of God's name, the pursuit continues. Prayer opens the door between heaven and earth in your life.

An Entire Region Chases Jesus

After Jesus fed five thousand men, with additional women and children, in Mark 6, he sent his disciples ahead across the sea while he "went up on the mountain to pray" (v. 46). It is highly likely Jesus received direction from his Father through prayer for what would happen next. This is what a constant yes, similar to the one that brought those little bottles of Coca-Cola to the desolate road on the volcano, looked like in the life of Jesus. Jesus was passionately interdependent on the Father while on his sacred chase.

After prayer, Jesus took the road less traveled and walked on the water to meet his disciples. They were struggling against the wind, but as soon as Jesus got into the boat with them, the wind ceased (v. 51). It usually happens that way. What once terrified us or distracted us bows its knee to the One who is greater than all. Sometimes, every now and then, God allows the storm to rage a little while longer (Acts 27). Either way, God reigns over each and every storm.

Once the boat came to shore, Jesus again set foot in the region of Gadara, where the very people lived whose swine had been destroyed and who had asked him to leave in Mark 5:17.

> When they had crossed over, they came to land at Gennesaret and moored to the shore. And when they got out of the boat, the people immediately recognized him and ran about the whole region and began to bring the sick people on their beds to wherever they heard he was. And wherever he came, in villages, cities, or countryside, they laid the sick in the marketplaces and implored him that they might touch even the fringe of his garment. And as many as touched it were made well. (Mark 6:53–56)

Jesus received a very different welcome from the people this time. Why? Those who previously rejected Jesus had begun their sacred chase too. No one walked up to Jesus and said, "Sir, I remember you. You were there when the creepy guy put on some clothes. You killed my pigs. I still haven't forgotten that day." No, that's not at all what happened. When Jesus came back, they started numbering their days.

I picture it going something like this: "Excuse me, sir, but I remember you. Unfortunately, I kicked you out of my neighborhood because I thought it was strange and weird when the naked, bloody, insane man we called Legion all of a sudden experienced a significant life change. I didn't exchange my normal for yours. I remember watching him sit there, the first time I ever witnessed that, by the way, and he was clothed. Dignity seemed to cover him like a wool blanket in winter, and his face glowed with peace like a little child's. It bothered me when my routine in life was disrupted as I watched the swine run down the steep bank. I didn't know how to handle it. No, I didn't want to. I thought Legion was out of his mind, but now I realize you were simply out of mine. It's almost as if you brought a new world to this one. Rather than surrendering, I argued and begged you to leave. And you did."

I can imagine the love in the eyes of Jesus in this moment. Jesus didn't think, *Yeah, you really blew it. I told you so!* No, I picture Jesus waiting there, looking at the townspeople with that same all-consuming gaze that drew the one they called Legion out of his cave to run toward the Love that pulled heaven and earth together. Then one of them would say, "We asked you to leave, and you did, but we are so glad you sent him back home. He came and told us about how merciful God is, and the irresistible mercy took our hardened hearts and softened them like the warmth from a hand does the clay. As soon as we saw you glance our way, we knew we just had to do whatever it took to get everyone within your reach. I told the kids to run and tell everyone that Love had come back."

And they did.

They didn't walk, crawl, or casually meander around the area. They passionately ran all over. This time, rather than being expelled for performing one miracle that started with a glance, Jesus walked up and down the dusty road with the sick and hurting on each side. They were laid at his feet by those who pressed in to be closer to him, those whose sacred chase was made possible by God's mercy.

The only evidence we have in the Gospels as to why Jesus received a very different welcome in this area the second time he came is because the man who was set free from the darkness dared to simply *go home*. The kingdom of God invades earth when we do the seemingly little things with a heart fully connected and devoted to God.

I cannot find a reliable source for whatever happened to the unnamed man they called Legion who started the chase of a lifetime with Jesus. I do know the Romans came to Jerusalem approximately thirty-five years after the events in Mark 6, when the roads of the Decapolis were lined with people who were amazed at Jesus. I wrote about it briefly in *Grace in the Valley*.

The Zealots, a group of radicalized religious followers, had finally pushed the Roman government to a point of no return through their guerrilla-style attacks. Continuous rebellion in Jerusalem lured the Roman soldiers into the city around AD 67. The Jews and Christians who remained within the city of Jerusalem were swept up in the chaos and would endure torture and murder. Some fled in order to spare the lives of their family.

I was told by scholars and some historians in Israel that the Christians who escaped from Jerusalem during this time were rejected by the surrounding regions for fear of the same fate falling upon them. In essence, they became refugees in their homeland. Their love for God was strong and they refused to worship Caesar, as was ordered. The Christians were turned away by every region except one: Gadara.

Decades after Jesus changed the man's life and healed his heart, as he lived a life marked by spiritual passion, the power of that one glance still endured. Your decisive action to accept God's invitation to inherit all that Jesus died on the cross to give you does the same. One of the most amazing things about God is that our inheritance is not only immeasurable and eternal but *accessible*. A heart's cry directed toward God in total surrender continues to echo from generation to generation. The sound is heard when a parent passionately cries out in prayer or when the power of compassion is demonstrated in a world soaked in desperation. It is revealed when we align our actions with God's best even when it costs us something—or even everything.

You will never regret starting and finishing your sacred chase. In the end, we are as close to God as we want to be. The new normal, and only normal for that matter, is Jesus.

Let us crucify every excuse, and then let us begin the sacred chase.

It is the opportunity of a lifetime and for all of eternity.

Notes

Chapter 1 Beyond Belief

1. Antonella Lazzeri, "If I Hadn't Spotted That the Sea Was Fizzing Then My Parents, Sister and Me Would All Be Dead Says Tilly Smith," *The Sun*, December 26, 2014, https://www.thesun.co.uk/archives/news/635504/if-i-hadnt -spotted-that-the-sea-was-fizzing-then-my-parents-sister-and-me-would-all -be-dead/; "This Day in History, December 26 2004: Tsunami Devastates Indian Ocean Coast," History, July 28, 2019, https://www.history.com/this -day-in-history/tsunami-devastates-indian-ocean-coast.

2. "2222: Zóé," Bible Hub, accessed August 29, 2019, https://biblehub.com /greek/2222.htm.

3. "4053: Perissos," Bible Hub, accessed October 8, 2019, https://bible hub.com/greek/4053.htm.

4. Joseph T. Hallinan, "The Remarkable Power of Hope," *Kidding Ourselves* (blog), May 7, 2014, https://www.psychologytoday.com/us/blog/kid ding-ourselves/201405/the-remarkable-power-hope.

5. "1411: Dunamis," Bible Hub, accessed October 8, 2019, https://bible hub.com/greek/1411.htm.

6. "1754: Energió," Bible Hub, accessed August 29, 2019, https://biblehub .com/greek/1754.htm.

7. Henri Nouwen, *With Open Hands* (Notre Dame: Ave Maria Press, 1995), 36.

8. "73: Agón," Bible Hub, accessed August 29, 2019, https://biblehub.com /greek/73.htm.

9. "266: Hamartia," Bible Hub, accessed August 29, 2019, https://biblehub .com/greek/266.htm.

Chapter 2 Stained Glass and Starry Nights

1. Eugene Peterson, *The Jesus Way* (Grand Rapids: Eerdmans, 2007), 230.

2. "Metanoia," Bible Study Tools, accessed October 8, 2019, https://www.biblestudytools.com/lexicons/greek/nas/metanoia.html.

3. For more information, see Rodney Stark, *The Rise of Christianity: How the Obscure, Marginal Jesus Movement Became the Dominant Religious Force in the Western World in a Few Centuries* (New York: HarperCollins, 1997), 73–84.

4. Richard Rohr, "Jesus' Alternative Reality," Center for Action and Contemplation, January 18, 2018, https://cac.org/jesus-alternative-reality-2018-01-18/.

5. "The Starry Night, 1889 by Vincent Van Gogh," vincentvangogh.org, accessed September 3, 2019, https://www.vincentvangogh.org/starry-night.jsp.

6. Makoto Fujimura, "'The Starry Night': Biola University Commencement Address, May, 2012," Makoto Fujimura, May 26, 2012, https://www.makotofujimura.com/writings/the-starry-night-biola-university-commencement-address-may-2012/.

7. Cliff Edwards, *van Gogh and God: A Creative Spiritual Quest* (Chicago: Loyola, 1989), 70.

8. Fujimura, "'The Starry Night.'"

9. "The Starry Night," MoMA Learning, accessed September 4, 2019, https://www.moma.org/learn/moma_learning/vincent-van-gogh-the-starry-night-1889/.

10. "691: To Theo van Gogh, on or about Saturday, 29 September 1888," *Vincent van Gogh: The Letters*, accessed October 8, 2019, http://www.vangoghletters.org/vg/letters/let691/letter.html#translation.

Chapter 3 God Welcomes You . . . Wherever You Are

1. Leslie Maryann Neal, "How Photojournalism Killed Kevin Carter," ATI, September 7, 2014, https://allthatsinteresting.com/kevin-carter; Bill Keller, "Kevin Carter, a Pulitzer Winner for Sudan Photo, Is Dead at 33," *New York Times*, July 29, 1994, https://www.nytimes.com/1994/07/29/world/kevin-carter-a-pulitzer-winner-for-sudan-photo-is-dead-at-33.html; Eamonn McCabe, "From the Archive, 30 July 1994: Photojournalist Kevin Carter Dies," *The Guardian*, July 30, 2014, https://www.theguardian.com/media/2014/jul/30/kevin-carter-photojournalist-obituary-archive-1994.

2. John Dear, "The School of Prophets," *On the Road to Peace* (blog), November 17, 2009, https://www.ncronline.org/blogs/road-peace/school-prophets.

3. Keller, "Kevin Carter, a Pulitzer Winner for Sudan Photo, Is Dead at 33."

4. Scott Macleod, "The Life and Death of Kevin Carter," *Time*, June 24, 2001, http://content.time.com/time/magazine/article/0,9171,165071,00.html.

5. Michael Harris, "Bereshit," *The JC*, October 19, 2011, https://www.thejc.com/judaism/sidrah/bereshit-1.28398?highlight=genesis+2%3A7.

6. "Brené Brown Quotes," Goodreads, accessed October 8, 2019, https://www.goodreads.com/quotes/417396-we-cultivate-love-when-we-allow-our-most-vulnerable-and.

7. Dorothy Sayers, "The Greatest Drama Ever Staged," *Christian Letters to a Post-Christian World: A Selection of Essays* (Grand Rapids: Eerdmans, 1969), 15.

8. "2770: Kerdainó," Bible Hub, accessed October 8, 2019, https://biblehub.com/strongs/greek/2770.htm.

9. George Orwell, "George Orwell Quotes," *Goodreads*, accessed September 4, 2019, https://www.goodreads.com/quotes/335549-reading-mr-malcolm-muggeridge-s-brilliant-and-depressing-book-the-thirties.

10. "5590: Psuché," Bible Hub, accessed October 8, 2019, https://biblehub.com/greek/5590.htm.

11. "Entry for Strong's #2588—Kardiá," Study Light, accessed October 8, 2019, https://www.studylight.org/lexicons/greek/2588.html.

12. "Strong's G4151—Pneuma," Blue Letter Bible, accessed October 8, 2019, https://www.blueletterbible.org/lang/lexicon/lexicon.cfm?t=kjv&strongs=g4151.

13. "Strong's #2222: Zoe," Bible Tools, accessed October 8, 2019, https://www.bibletools.org/index.cfm/fuseaction/Lexicon.show/ID/G2222/zoe.htm.

14. Roger Knapp, "Special Olympics," RogerKnapp.com, accessed October 8, 2019, https://www.rogerknapp.com/inspire/olympics.htm.

Chapter 4 Legion's Greatest Treasure

1. Seth Borenstein, "Scientists Witness Huge Cosmic Crash, Find Origins of Gold," *Chicago Tribune*, October 16, 2017, https://www.chicagotribune.com/news/nationworld/science/ct-neutron-star-collision-20171016-story.html.

2. Charlotte Wold, "The Number of Millionaires Continues to Increase," Investopedia, October 15, 2018, https://www.investopedia.com/news/number-millionaires-continues-increase/.

3. Catherine Clifford, "There Are a Record 2,208 Billionaires in the World, according to Forbes' 2018 Rich List," CNBC, March 7, 2018, https://www.cnbc.com/2018/03/07/forbes-there-are-a-record-2208-billionaires-in-the-world.html.

4. Daniel Honan, "The First Trillionaires Will Make Their Fortunes in Space," Big Think, May 2, 2011, https://bigthink.com/think-tank/the-first-trillionaires-will-make-their-fortunes-in-space.

5. "Ancient Gadara City of Philosophers," University of Haifa, accessed September 4, 2019, http://research.haifa.ac.il/~mluz/gadara.folder/gadara2.html.

6. "Ancient Gadara City of Philosophers."

7. Larry W. Hurtado, *Mark* (Peabody, MA: Hendrickson, 1989), 71.

8. Ed Murphy, *The Handbook for Spiritual Warfare*, rev. ed. (Nashville: Thomas Nelson, 2003), 566.

9. "Ancient Jewish Cities & Regions: Gadara," Jewish Virtual Library, accessed September 5, 2019, https://www.jewishvirtuallibrary.org/gadara.

10. "Mark 5:4," Bible Hub, accessed September 5, 2019, https://biblehub.com/parallel/mark/5-4.htm.

11. Joachim Jeremias, *The Proclamation of Jesus* (New York: Scribner, 1971), 85–96.

12. William Barclay, "The Gospel of Mark," *The Daily Study Bible* (Philadelphia: Westminster, 1958), 116–18.

13. Victor Hugo, *Les Miserables* (New York: Carleton, Madison Square, 1862), 46.

14. Avi Selk, "A Man Nearly Jumped off an Overpass. 13 Truckers Made a Safety Net," *Washington Post*, April 24, 2018, https://www.washingtonpost.com/news/inspired-life/wp/2018/04/24/a-man-nearly-jumped-off-an-overpass-13-truckers-made-a-safety-net/?noredirect=on&utm_term=.996650bc5308.

Chapter 5 You Travel Not Alone

1. Robert D. McFadden, "Nicholas Winton, Rescuer of 669 Children from Holocaust, Dies at 106," *New York Times*, July 1, 2015, https://www.nytimes.com/2015/07/02/world/europe/nicholas-winton-is-dead-at-106-saved-children-from-the-holocaust.html.

2. "Sir Nicholas Winton—BBC Programme 'That's Life' Aired in 1988," YouTube video, 1:39, uploaded by aggy007, September 1, 2009, https://www.youtube.com/watch?v=6_nFuJAF5F0.

3. McFadden, "Nicholas Winton."

4. "1980: Halak," Bible Hub, accessed October 8, 2019, https://biblehub.com/hebrew/1980.htm.

5. Søren Kierkegaard, *Kierkegaard's Writings XXIII, Volume 23: The Moment and Late Writings* (Princeton: Princeton University Press, 1998), 308.

6. Chip Grabow and Lisa Rose, "The US Has Had 57 Times as Many School Shootings as the Other Major Industrialized Nations Combined," CNN, May 21, 2018, https://www.cnn.com/2018/05/21/us/school-shooting-us-versus-world-trnd/index.html.

7. Katherine Lam, "Nikolas Cruz 'School Shooter' Comment Reported to FBI Months Ago, Vlogger Says," Fox News, February 15, 2018, https://www.foxnews.com/us/nikolas-cruz-school-shooter-comment-reported-to-fbi-months-ago-vlogger-says.

8. Travis Fedschun, "Grandmother Thwarted Washington School Shooting by Looking at Student's Journal, Cops Say," Fox News, February 15, 2018, https://www.foxnews.com/us/grandmother-thwarted-washington-school-shooting-by-looking-at-students-journal-cops-say.

9. "6223: Ashir," Bible Hub, accessed October 8, 2019, https://biblehub.com/strongs/hebrew/6223.htm.

10. "7326: Rush," Bible Hub, accessed October 8, 2019, https://biblehub.com/hebrew/7326.htm.

11. "3535: Kibsah or Kabsah," Bible Hub, accessed October 8, 2019, https://biblehub.com/strongs/hebrew/3535.htm.

12. "1323: Bath," Bible Hub, accessed October 8, 2019, https://biblehub.com/hebrew/1323.htm.

13. "1982: Helek," Bible Hub, accessed October 8, 2019, https://biblehub.com/hebrew/1982.htm.

14. "2 Samuel 12:4," Bible Hub, accessed September 5, 2019, https://biblehub.com/commentaries/2_samuel/12-4.htm.

Chapter 6 God Speaks a Better Word

1. "3478: Yisrael," Bible Hub, accessed October 8, 2019, https://biblehub.com/hebrew/3478.htm.

2. "7307: Ruach," Bible Hub, accessed October 8, 2019, https://biblehub.com/hebrew/7307.htm.

3. Joseph Meehan, "The Godfather of the Navy SEALs," Huckberry, February 23, 2016, https://huckberry.com/journal/posts/the-godfather-of-the-navy-seals?noch1.

4. *Merriam-Webster*, s.v. "accusation," Merriam-Webster.com, accessed September 5, 2019, https://www.merriam-webster.com/dictionary/accusation.

Chapter 7 When Demons Beg

1. A. B. Bruce, "The Synoptic Gospels," in *The Expositor's Greek Testament*, vol. 1, ed. W. Robertson Nicoll (Grand Rapids: Eerdmans, 1956), 372.

2. "Fun Flea Facts," Health24, March 10, 2011, https://www.health24.com/Lifestyle/Pet-Health/Your-pets-health/Fun-flea-facts-20120721.

3. True Activist, "Is This How We Are Forced to View the World in a Certain Way?" True Activist, April 15, 2015, http://www.trueactivist.com/is-this-how-we-are-forced-to-view-the-world-in-a-certain-way-t1/.

4. Ester Buchholz, "The Call of Solitude," *Psychology Today*, January 1, 1998, https://www.psychologytoday.com/us/articles/199801/the-call-solitude.

5. "2403: Chatta'ah," Bible Hub, accessed October 8, 2019, https://biblehub.com/hebrew/2403.htm.

6. "5771: Avon," Bible Hub, accessed October 8, 2019, https://biblehub.com/hebrew/5771.htm.

Chapter 8 The Dove Remains

1. Alfred Mehran, *The Terminal Man* (London: Corgi, 2004).

2. Kara Goldfarb, "This Man Got Stuck at the Airport for 18 Years," ATI, May 21, 2018, https://allthatsinteresting.com/mehran-karimi-nasseri.

3. "H7307," Hebrew Dictionary (Lexicon-Concordance), accessed October 8, 2019, http://lexiconcordance.com/hebrew/7307.html.

Chapter 9 A New Normal

1. "5399: Phobeó," Bible Hub, accessed September 5, 2019, https://biblehub.com/greek/5399.htm.

2. "Amy Carmichael Helped the Helpless," Christianity.com, July 16, 2010, https://www.christianity.com/church/church-history/church-history-for -kids/amy-carmichael-helped-the-helpless-11634859.html.

3. "Some Quotes from Missionary Amy Carmichael," *Abundantly Pardoned* (blog), May 23, 2012, https://abundantlypardoned.wordpress.com/2012 /05/23/some-quotes-from-missionary-amy-carmichael/.

4. "Some Quotes from Missionary Amy Carmichael."

5. Robert C. Ford, Michael C. Sturman, and Cherrill P. Heaton, *Managing Quality Service in Hospitality: How Organizations Achieve Excellence in the Guest Experience* (New York: Delmar, 2012), 332.

6. "Whatever Happened to the Twelve Apostles?" Christianity.com, April 28, 2010, https://www.christianity.com/church/church-history/timeline/1-300 /whatever-happened-to-the-twelve-apostles-11629558.html.

Chapter 10 Go Home

1. Journey Staff, "Our Story 1886–1892: The Beginning," Coca-Cola Journey, accessed September 5, 2019, https://www.coca-cola.co.uk/stories/our -story-1886-1892--the-beginning.

2. Journey Staff, "Our Story 1919–1940: Coke's First Olympics," Coca-Cola Journey, accessed September 5, 2019, https://www.coca-cola.co.uk/sto ries/history/heritage/our-story-1919-1940--cokes-first-olympics.

3. Lara O'Reilly, "15 Mind-Blowing Facts about Coca-Cola," *Business Insider*, September 25, 2015, https://www.businessinsider.com/facts-about -coca-cola-2015-9.

4. Journey Staff, "Coca-Cola Fun Facts," Coca-Cola Journey, accessed September 5, 2019, https://www.coca-cola.co.uk/stories/coca-cola-fun-facts -infographic.

5. "A State of Innovation: The Coca-Cola Company," Georgia Historical Society, accessed September 5, 2019, https://georgiahistory.com/a-state-of -innovation-the-coca-cola-company/.

6. "4487: Manah," Bible Hub, accessed September 5, 2019, https://bible hub.com/hebrew/4487.htm.

7. "3117: Yom," Bible Hub, accessed September 5, 2019, https://biblehub .com/hebrew/3117.htm.

8. "3045: Yada," Bible Hub, accessed October 8, 2019, https://biblehub .com/strongs/hebrew/3045.htm.

9. Doug Alexander, "Cryptocurrency CEO Dies, and No One Else Knows Passwords to Unlock Millions in Customer Coins," *Chicago Tribune*, February 5, 2019, https://www.chicagotribune.com/business/ct-biz-quadrigacx -cryptocurrency-passwords-20190205-story.html.

10. "Catholic Encyclopedia: Miracle," Catholic Online, accessed October 8, 2019, https://www.catholic.org/encyclopedia/view.php?id=8016.

Heath Adamson (PhD, University of London) is the author of *Grace in the Valley*. His life was changed dramatically when, at the age of seventeen, he was rescued out of a life steeped in drug abuse and the occult. Now a sought-after speaker at conferences, seminars, universities, and churches, Adamson seeks to bring audiences from simply knowing information about God to actually experiencing God in life-changing ways. He and his wife, Ali, and their two daughters, Leighton and Dallon, believe you are God's favorite place to be.

Finding INTIMACY with God through Psalm 23

Awakening to God's Presence
When He Feels Far Away

GRACE
in the
VALLEY

HEATH ADAMSON

Connect with

BakerBooks
Relevant. Intelligent. Engaging.

Sign up for announcements about new and upcoming titles at

BakerBooks.com/SignUp

@ReadBakerBooks

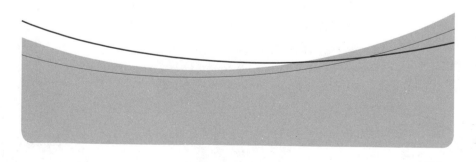